# THE
# LOW-FAT INDIAN
## COOKBOOK

# THE
# LOW–FAT INDIAN
## COOKBOOK

DELICIOUS AND AUTHENTIC INDIAN RECIPES
FOR HEALTHY LIVING

# SHEHZAD HUSAIN

SMITHMARK

*Bismillah – Hir – Rahmaan – Nir – Raheem*

For my sister Shehnaz, with love and affection.

This edition published in 1994 by
SMITHMARK Publishers Inc.
16 East 32nd Street
New York, NY 10016

SMITHMARK books are available for bulk purchase,
for sales promotion and premium use. For details
write or call the manager of special sales,
SMITHMARK Publishers Inc., 16 East 32nd Street,
New York, NY 10016; (212) 532-6600.

© 1994 Anness Publishing Limited
1 Boundary Row
London SE1 8HP

ISBN 0-8317-1303-8

Editorial Director: Joanna Lorenz
Project Editor: Judith Simons
Designer: David Rowley
Jacket Design: Peter Butler
Photographer: David Armstrong
Stylist: Blake Minton
Home Economist (steps): Shehzad Husain
Home Economist (finished dishes): Steven Wheeler
Nutritional data: Wendy Doyle

Typeset by MC Typeset Limited
Printed and bound in Singapore

MEASUREMENTS

Three sets of equivalent measurements have been provided in the
recipes here, in the following order: Metric, Imperial and
American. It is essential that units of measurement are not mixed
within each recipe. Where conversions result in awkward numbers,
these have been rounded for convenience, but are accurate enough
to produce successful results.

NOTE

The nutritional analyses accompanying each recipe were prepared
using a computer program called FOODBASE which is based on
data from McCance & Widdowson's *The Composition of Foods*, with
fatty acid data from The Institute of Brain Chemistry and Human
Nutrition. Ingredients specified as optional have not been included
in the related analysis, and where weights have not been given in
the recipes an approximate value has been calculated.

PICTURE CREDITS

The publishers would like to thank the following for additional
pictures: jacket photograph of author © Tony Isbitt; pages 10, 11,
22, 23, 42, 43, 54, 55, 68, 69, 80, 81, 88, 89 © Pankaj Shah.

# Contents

# Introduction

DELICIOUS food, prepared and served with care, and consumed with relish is one of life's pleasures, and by adhering to a few simple dietary guidelines you can be sure too that what you eat is also good for you. There is now widespread agreement on healthy eating and the message is fairly straightforward. Eat less fat, especially saturated fat, less sugar, less salt and more fibre. Loosely translated, this means eating more vegetables, fruit, complex carbohydrate foods such as rice, bread and pasta (preferably unrefined or wholegrain varieties), more fish, leaner meats, and poultry without skin. With all these pleasurable foods to choose from, healthy eating should never be regarded as dull or uninteresting, but a pleasure to cook and a joy to eat.

Looking at these recommended foods it is surprising that Indian cooking is generally considered to be unhealthy. In fact, good Indian cuisine will always make use of lean, trimmed meat, poultry is never cooked with the skin, and several regions on the subcontinent are famed for their delicious fish and seafood dishes. A wide variety of fresh vegetables and wholefoods, such as lentils and pulses, are integral to Indian cooking and every meal is served with either rice or bread, and sometimes both. However, until more recent times, Indian cooks always used liberal quantities of pure ghee (clarified butter) for frying. Now, as more people are aware of the importance of reducing the fat content in their diet, they are happily settling for vegetable oils for all their cooking.

The changes in diet promoted here are therefore not designed to be dramatic. The amount of vegetable oil used for cooking has been greatly reduced, and low or reduced fat ingredients have been specified wherever possible. In particular, I have tried to reduce the more unhealthy type of fat – saturated fat – which comes principally from animal sources such as dairy foods and fatty meats. Every gram of fat provides 9 kilocalories – more than twice the number from 1 gram of protein or carbohydrate. Therefore, for those concerned about calorie intakes, there is the added advantage that in lowering the fat content of traditional recipes, the calorie content will also be reduced considerably. Experts recommend that no more than 30–33 per cent of our calories should come from fat. Based on a 2000 kilocalorie diet this means reducing the amount of fat from approximately 100 grams a day to 67–70 grams. We have chosen to take one-fifth of that amount (14 grams) as a cut-off point for one serving of all the recipes in this book.

I have tried to make the recipes as simple and uncomplicated as possible, allowing you to enjoy these dishes any time of the week. I also hope to show you that the fat content of traditional recipes can be easily and effectively reduced without sacrificing the exotic flavours and aromas of Indian fare, so you can enjoy many delicious Indian meals without guilt. I wish you happy and healthy eating.

*Shehzad Husain*

## Cooking Equipment

You should find that your own kitchen is well equipped with everything you need to produce the dishes in this book. Good-quality saucepans with heavy bases, and wooden spoons and a slotted spoon to use with them, mixing bowls, sharp knives, a chopping board, a sieve (strainer) and a rolling pin are the main essentials. A balloon whisk for beating yogurt and a pastry brush for basting kebabs (kabobs) with marinade may also be useful for some of the recipes.

A heavy-based frying pan (skillet) is a must, and you may like to try cooking some of the dishes in a traditional Indian karahi, a deep, round-bottomed vessel with two circular carrying handles. Karahis are very sturdy and therefore capable of withstanding high cooking temperatures and sizzling oils. Wooden stands are available, too, so the pans can be brought to the table to serve. The other specialist cooking vessel used in the Indian kitchen is a tava, a flat cast-iron frying pan used for cooking chapatis and other breads and for roasting spices, but any sturdy frying pan can be substituted.

A food processor or blender is a great labour-saving tool and will be invaluable for making pastes or puréeing ingredients. Whole spices can be freshly ground using a mortar and pestle, or, if you have one, a coffee grinder makes the job so much easier.

## Cooking Tips

● The final colour and texture of a curry depend on how well you brown the onions in the first stage of cooking. This requires patience, especially as you will be cooking them in small quantities of oil. Heat the oil first, add the onions, then reduce the heat slightly. Only stir the onions occasionally; excessive stirring will draw the moisture from them which will inhibit the browning process.

## Useful Equipment

**1** *food processor* **2** *balloon whisk* **3** *heavy-based saucepans* **4** *heavy-based frying pan (skillet)* **5** *mixing bowls* **6** *sieve (strainer)* **7** *karahi* **8** *pastry brush* **9** *sharp knives* **10** *slotted spoon* **11** *wooden spoons* **12** *rolling pin* **13** *mortar and pestle* **14** *coffee grinder* **15** *tava*

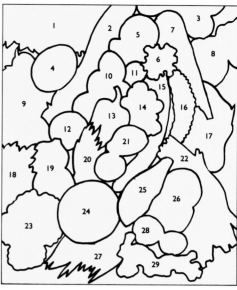

## Fresh Produce

*Fresh vegetables, herbs, fruits and spices are a must in Indian cooking. This is just a selection of those used in the recipes and includes some of the exotic-looking vegetables you might see in Asian stores.*

**1** *fresh fenugreek* **2** *mooli (white radish)* **3** *tomatoes* **4** *ripe mango* **5** *onion* **6** *fresh mint* **7** *kaddoo or doodi – similar to pumpkin* **8** *green (bell) pepper* **9** *fresh green chillies* **10** *green or raw (unripe) mango* **11** *garlic* **12** *red onion* **13** *red (bell) pepper* **14** *cherry tomatoes* **15** *thurai – a courgette-like Indian vegetable* **16** *karela (bitter gourd)* **17** *small aubergines (eggplants)* **18** *fresh coriander (cilantro)* **19** *pomegranate* **20** *French (green) beans* **21** *lemons* **22** *spring onions (scallions)* **23** *cauliflower florets (flowerets)* **24** *okra* **25** *sweet potato* **26** *mushrooms* **27** *baby carrots* **28** *limes* **29** *ginger*

● Natural (plain) low-fat yogurt is used in many of the recipes as a healthy alternative to cream. It is a wonderful tenderizer and gives curries a thick, creamy texture. Always beat the yogurt with a fork first and then add it to the pan gradually, stirring continuously, to prevent it curdling.

● Some recipes specify whole spices, such as cinnamon sticks, cardamom pods and cloves. If wished, remove these from the dish before serving.

● There is no substitute for fresh coriander (cilantro) and the more used the better as it imparts a beautiful aroma and flavour. Happily, coriander is now readily available from most supermarkets, and more economically from Asian stores. If wished, buy a large quantity and freeze whatever you don't need. Simply cut off the roots and any thick stalks, wash the leaves in cold water and leave to drain in a sieve (strainer). When dry, chop and store in plastic bags or airtight containers in the freezer. Do not defrost before using.

## A Question of Taste

The spices used in a dish are integral to its flavour and aroma. One spice can completely alter the taste of a dish and a combination of several will also effect its colour and texture. The quantities of spices and salt specified in this book are merely a guide, so feel free to experiment and increase and decrease these as you wish.

This is particularly true of chilli powder and fresh and dried chillies; some brands and varieties are hotter than others. Experiment with quantities, adding less than specified, if wished. Much of the severe heat of fresh chillies is contained in the seeds, and these can be removed by splitting the chillies down the middle and washing them away under cold running water. You can also remove the seeds from dried chillies. Wash your hands thoroughly with soap and water after handling cut chillies and avoid touching your face – particularly your lips and eyes – for a good while afterwards.

## Home-Made Paneer

Paneer is a white, smooth-textured Indian cheese, available from some Asian stores. It appears in several of the low-fat recipes in this book and is quite easy to make at home, as follows. Bring 1 litre/1¾ pints/4 cups milk to the boil over a low heat. Add 2 tbsp lemon juice, stirring continuously and gently until the milk thickens and begins to curdle. Strain the curdled milk through a sieve (strainer) lined with muslin (cheesecloth). Set aside under a heavy weight for 1½–2 hours to press it into a flat shape about 1 cm/½ in thick. Cut and use as required; it will keep for about one week in the refrigerator.

## Making Ginger and Garlic Pulp

Ginger and garlic pulp is specified in many of the recipes here and it can be time-consuming to peel and process these everytime. It's much easier to make the pulps in large quantities and use as needed. The method is the same for both ingredients. The pulp can be stored in an airtight container or jar in the refrigerator for four to six weeks. Alternatively, freeze in ice-cube trays kept for the purpose (the pulps will taint the trays slightly). Add 1 tsp of the pulp to each compartment, freeze, remove from the tray and store in the freezer in a plastic bag.

1 Take about 225 g/8 oz ginger or garlic and soak overnight – this softens the skins and makes them easy to peel. Peel and place in a food processor or blender.

2 Process until pulped, adding a little water to get the right consistency, if necessary.

## Home-Made Garam Masala

For an ultra-fresh, home-made variety, grind together the following spices in a coffee grinder.

*4 × 2.5 cm/1 in cinnamon sticks*
*3 cloves*
*3 black peppercorns*
*2 black cardamom pods, with husks removed*
*2 tsp black cumin seeds*

## Glossary of Special Ingredients

**Almonds** Blanched almonds are available whole, flaked (slivered) and ground, and impart a sumptuous richness to curries. They are considered a great delicacy in India, where they are extremely expensive.

**Basmati rice** If possible, try to use basmati rice for all savoury rice dishes – the delicate flavour is unbeatable.

**Bay leaves** The large dried leaves of the bay laurel tree are one of the oldest herbs used in cookery.

**Cardamom pods** This spice is native to India, where it is considered to be the most prized spice after saffron. The pods can be used whole or the husks can be removed to release the seeds, and they have a slightly pungent but very aromatic taste. They come in three varieties: green, white and black. The green and white pods can be used for both sweet and savoury dishes or to flavour rice. The black pods are used only for savoury dishes.

**Cashew nuts** These full-flavoured nuts are a popular ingredient in many kinds of Asian cooking.

**Chana dhal** This is a round split yellow lentil, similar in appearance to the smaller moong dhal and the larger yellow split pea, which can be used as a substitute. It is used as a binding agent in some dishes and is widely available from Asian stores.

**Chapati flour** This is a type of wholemeal (whole-wheat) flour available from Asian stores and is used to make chapatis and other breads. Ordinary wholemeal flour can be used as a substitute if well sifted.

**Chick-peas (garbanzos)** This nutty tasting pulse is widely used in Indian vegetarian dishes.

**Chillies – dried red** These hot peppers are extremely fiery and should be used with caution. The heat can be toned down by removing the seeds before use. Dried chillies can be used whole or coarsely crushed.

**Chilli powder** Also known as cayenne pepper, this fiery ground spice should be used with caution. The heat varies from brand to brand, so adjust quantities to suit your tastebuds.

**Cinnamon** One of the earliest known spices, cinnamon has an aromatic and sweet flavour. It is sold ready-ground and as sticks.

**Cloves** This spice is used to flavour many sweet and savoury dishes and is usually added whole.

**Coconut** Used to flavour both sweet and savoury dishes, fresh coconut is now frequently available from supermarkets. Desiccated (shredded) coconut and creamed coconut make acceptable substitutes for most dishes.

**Coriander – fresh (cilantro)** This beautifully fragrant herb is used both in cooking and sprinkled over dishes as an attractive garnish.

**Coriander seeds** This aromatic spice has a pungent, slightly lemony flavour. The seeds are used widely, either coarsely ground or in powdered form, in meat, fish and poultry dishes. Ground coriander, a brownish powder, is an important constituent of any mixture of curry spices.

**Cumin** 'White' cumin seeds are oval, ridged and greenish brown in colour. They have a strong aroma and flavour and can be used whole or ground. Ready-ground cumin powder is widely available. Black cumin seeds are dark and aromatic and are used to flavour curries and rice.

**Curry leaves** Similar in appearance to bay leaves but with a very different flavour, these can be bought dried and occasionally fresh from Asian stores. Fresh leaves freeze well.

**Fennel seeds** Very similar in appearance to cumin seeds, fennel seeds have a very sweet taste and are used to flavour certain curries. They can also be chewed as a mouth-freshener after a spicy meal.

**Fenugreek – fresh** Sold in bunches, this herb has very small leaves and is used to flavour both meat and vegetarian dishes. Always discard the stalks, which will impart a bitterness to a dish if used.

**Fenugreek seeds** These flat seeds are extremely pungent and slightly bitter.

**Garam masala** This is a mixture of spices which can be made from freshly ground spices at home or purchased ready-made. There is no set recipe, but a typical mixture might include black cumin seeds, peppercorns, cloves, cinnamon and black cardamon pods.

**Garlic** This is a standard ingredient, along with ginger, in most curries. It can be used pulped, crushed or chopped. Whole cloves are sometimes added to dishes.

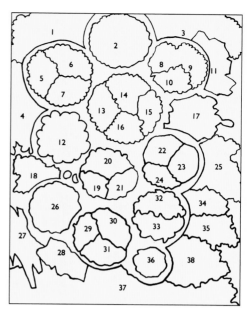

## Dried Ingredients

*These are just some of the dried spices, fruits, lentils, pulses, seeds, nuts and herbs that are used in Indian dishes.*

**1** *chick-peas (garbanzos)* **2** *chapati flour* **3** *sesame seeds* **4** *sultanas (golden raisins)* **5** *chana dhal (split yellow lentils)* **6** *toor dhal (split yellow lentils)* **7** *urid dhal, with hull (black gram)* **8** *coriander seeds* **9** *black peppercorns* **10** *green cardamom pods* **11** *creamed coconut* **12** *dried red chillies* **13** *urid dhal, dehulled (black gram)* **14** *moong dhal (small split yellow lentils)* **15** *pomegranate seeds* **16** *whole brown lentils* **17** *flaked (slivered) almonds* **18** *cloves* **19** *mango powder* **20** *turmeric* **21** *chilli powder* **22** *garam masala* **23** *onion seeds* **24** *fenugreek seeds* **25** *fennel seeds* **26** *desiccated (shredded) coconut* **27** *cinnamon sticks* **28** *bay leaves* **29** *ground coriander* **30** *black mustard seeds* **31** *ground cumin* **32** *peanuts* **33** *cashew nuts* **34** *black cumin seeds* **35** *white cumin seeds* **36** *mango chutney* **37** *basmati rice* **38** *ground almonds*

**Ginger** One of the most popular spices in India and also one of the oldest, fresh ginger is an important ingredient in many curries and is now widely available. Dried powdered ginger is a useful standby.

**Mangoes** Ripe fresh mangoes are used in sweet dishes, while green or unripe mangoes are sometimes used in curries and to make mango chutney. Mango powder is made from dried unripe mangoes and has a sour taste.

**Masoor dhal** These split red lentils are actually orange in colour and turn a pale yellow when cooked. Whole brown lentils are a type of red lentil with the husk intact.

**Moong dhal** This teardrop-shaped split yellow lentil is similar to, though smaller than, chana dhal.

**Mustard seeds – black** Round in shape and sharp in flavour, black mustard seeds are used for flavouring curries and pickles.

**Onion seeds** Black in colour and triangular in shape, these seeds are widely used in pickles and to flavour vegetable curries.

**Peppercorns** Black peppercorns are sometimes used whole with other whole spices, such as cloves, cardamon pods and bay leaves, to flavour curries. Otherwise, whenever possible, use freshly ground or crushed black pepper if the recipe calls for it.

**Pomegranate seeds** These can be extracted from fresh pomegranates or bought in jars from Asian stores and impart a delicious tangy flavour.

**Poppy seeds** These whole seeds are usually used toasted to bring out the full flavour.

**Saffron** The world's most expensive spice is the dried stigmas of the saffron crocus, which is native to Asia Minor. To produce 450 g/2 lb of saffron requires 60,000 stigmas. Fortunately, only a small quantity of saffron is needed to flavour and colour a dish, whether sweet or savoury. Saffron is sold as strands and in powder form, and has a beautiful flavour and aroma.

**Sesame seeds** Small, whole, cream-coloured seeds, these have a slightly nutty taste.

**Toor dhal** A shiny split yellow lentil, toor dhal is similar in size to chana dhal.

**Turmeric** This bright yellow, bitter-tasting spice is sold ground. It is used mainly for colour rather than flavour.

**Urid dhal** Also known as black gram, this lentil is similar in size to moong dhal and is available either with the blackish hull retained or removed.

*Opposite: Pasteurizing milk, a daily ritual in the home*
*Above: A spice market in Dehli*

# Appetizers & Snacks

*If you like to serve an Indian meal in several courses, Chicken Tikka, Chicken with Pineapple, or Tandoori Masala Spring Lamb Chops will make the ideal start to the menu — mouthwatering and light, they will awaken the appetite without being too filling. There are also ideas here for low-fat lunches or suppertime snacks, including a deliciously spicy filling for baked potatoes.*

# Tomato and Coriander (Cilantro) Soup

*Although soups are not often eaten in India or Pakistan, tomato soup seems to be among the most popular ones. It is excellent on a cold winter's day.*

**SERVES 4**

INGREDIENTS
*675 g/1½ lb tomatoes*
*2 tbsp vegetable oil*
*1 bay leaf*
*4 spring onions (scallions), chopped*
*1 tsp salt*
*½ tsp garlic pulp*
*1 tsp crushed black peppercorns*
*2 tbsp chopped fresh coriander (cilantro)*
*750 ml/1¼ pints/good 3 cups water*
*1 tbsp cornflour (cornstarch)*

**Garnish**
*1 spring onion (scallion), chopped (optional)*
*2 tbsp single (light) cream (optional)*

### NUTRITIONAL VALUES (per portion)

| | |
|---|---|
| Total fat | 7.16 g |
| Saturated fat | 1.37 g |
| Cholesterol | 2.80 mg |
| Energy (kcals/kj) | 113/474 |

1 ▲ To skin the tomatoes, plunge them in very hot water, then take them out more or less straight away. The skin should now peel off quickly and easily. Once this is done chop the tomatoes.

2 ▲ In a medium saucepan, heat the oil and fry the chopped tomatoes, bay leaf and chopped spring onions (scallions) for a few minutes until soft.

3 ▲ Gradually add the salt, garlic, peppercorns and fresh coriander (cilantro) to the tomato mixture, finally adding the water. Bring to the boil, lower the heat and simmer for 15–20 minutes.

4 Dissolve the cornflour (cornstarch) in a little water.

5 ▲ Remove the soup from the heat and press through a sieve (strainer).

6 ▲ Return to the pan, add the cornflour and stir over a gentle heat for about 3 minutes until thickened.

7 Pour into individual serving dishes and garnish with the chopped spring onion and cream, if using. Serve hot with bread.

### COOK'S TIP

*If the only fresh tomatoes available are rather pale and under-ripe, add 1 tbsp tomato purée (paste) to the pan with the chopped tomatoes to enhance the colour and flavour of the soup.*

# Chicken Naan Pockets

*This quick-and-easy dish is ideal for a quick snack lunch or supper and excellent as picnic fare. For speed, use the ready-to-bake naans available in some supermarkets and Asian stores, or try warmed pitta bread instead.*

**SERVES 4**

INGREDIENTS
*4 naan*
*3 tbsp natural (plain) low-fat yogurt*
*1¹/₂ tsp garam masala*
*1 tsp chilli powder*
*1 tsp salt*
*3 tbsp lemon juice*
*1 tbsp chopped fresh coriander (cilantro)*
*1 fresh green chilli, chopped*
*450 g/1 lb/3¹/₄ cups chicken, skinned, boned and cubed*
*1 tbsp vegetable oil (optional)*
*8 onion rings*
*2 tomatoes, quartered*
*¹/₂ white cabbage, shredded*

**Garnish**
*lemon wedges*
*2 small tomatoes, halved*
*mixed salad leaves*
*fresh coriander (cilantro)*

| NUTRITIONAL VALUES (per portion) | |
| --- | --- |
| Total fat | 10.85 g |
| Saturated fat | 3.01 g |
| Cholesterol | 65.64 mg |
| Energy (kcals/kj) | 364/1529 |

1 Cut into the middle of each naan to make a pocket, then set aside.

2 Mix together the yogurt, garam marsala, chilli powder, salt, lemon juice, fresh coriander (cilantro) and chopped green chilli. Pour the marinade over the chicken pieces and leave to marinate for about 1 hour.

3 After 1 hour preheat the grill (broiler) to very hot, then lower the heat to medium. Place the chicken in a flameproof dish and grill (broil) for 15–20 minutes until tender and cooked through, turning the chicken pieces at least twice. If wished, baste with the oil while cooking.

4 ▲ Remove from the heat and fill each naan with the chicken and then with the onion rings, tomatoes and cabbage. Serve with the garnish ingredients.

# Chicken Tikka

*This chicken dish is an extremely popular Indian appetizer and is quick and easy to cook. Chicken Tikka can also be served as a main course for four.*

**SERVES 6**

INGREDIENTS
*450 g/1 lb/3¹/₄ cups chicken, skinned, boned and cubed*
*1 tsp ginger pulp*
*1 tsp garlic pulp*
*1 tsp chilli powder*
*¹/₄ tsp turmeric*
*1 tsp salt*
*150 ml/¹/₄ pint/²/₃ cup natural (plain) low-fat yogurt*
*4 tbsp lemon juice*
*1 tbsp chopped fresh coriander (cilantro)*
*1 tbsp vegetable oil*

**Garnish**
*1 small onion, cut into rings*
*lime wedges*
*mixed salad*
*fresh coriander (cilantro)*

| NUTRITIONAL VALUES (per portion) | |
| --- | --- |
| Total fat | 5.50 g |
| Saturated fat | 1.47 g |
| Cholesterol | 44.07 mg |
| Energy (kcals/kj) | 131/552 |

1 In a medium bowl, mix together the chicken pieces, ginger, garlic, chilli powder, turmeric, salt, yogurt, lemon juice and fresh coriander (cilantro) and leave to marinate for at least 2 hours.

2 ▲ Place on a grill (broiler) tray or in a flameproof dish lined with foil and baste with the oil.

3 Preheat the grill to medium. Grill (broil) the chicken for 15–20 minutes until cooked, turning and basting 2–3 times. Serve with the garnish ingredients.

*Chicken Naan Pockets (top) and Chicken Tikka*

# Chicken with Pineapple

*This chicken has a delicate tang and is very tender. The pineapple not only tenderizes the chicken but also gives it a slight sweetness.*

**SERVES 6**

### INGREDIENTS
*225 g/8 oz/1 cup canned pineapple*
*1 tsp ground cumin*
*1 tsp ground coriander*
*½ tsp garlic pulp*
*1 tsp chilli powder*
*1 tsp salt*
*2 tbsp natural (plain) low-fat yogurt*
*1 tbsp chopped fresh coriander (cilantro)*
*few drops orange food colouring*
*275 g/10 oz/2 cups chicken, skinned and boned*
*½ red (bell) pepper*
*½ yellow or green (bell) pepper*
*1 large onion*
*6 cherry tomatoes*
*1 tbsp vegetable oil*

| NUTRITIONAL VALUES (per portion) | |
| --- | --- |
| Total fat | 6.72 g |
| Saturated fat | 1.51 g |
| Cholesterol | 40.63 mg |
| Energy (kcals/kj) | 170/716 |

**2 ▲** In a large mixing bowl, blend together the cumin, ground coriander, garlic, chilli powder, salt, yogurt, fresh coriander (cilantro) and food colouring, if using. Pour in the reserved pineapple juice and mix together.

**1 ▲** Drain the pineapple juice into a bowl. Reserve 8 large chunks of pineapple and squeeze the juice from the remaining chunks into the bowl and set aside. You should have about 120 ml/4 fl oz/½ cup of pineapple juice.

**3 ▲** Cut the chicken into bite-sized cubes, add to the yogurt and spice mixture and leave to marinate for about 1–1½ hours.

**4** Cut the (bell) peppers and onion into bite-sized chunks.

**5 ▲** Preheat the grill (broiler) to medium. Arrange the chicken pieces, vegetables and reserved pineapple chunks alternately on 6 wooden or metal skewers.

**6 ▲** Baste the kebabs (kabobs) with the oil, then place the skewers on a flameproof dish or grill tray. Grill (broil), turning and basting the chicken pieces with the marinade regularly, for about 15 minutes.

**7** Once the chicken pieces are cooked, remove them from the grill and serve either with salad or plain boiled rice.

### COOK'S TIP

*If possible, use a mixture of chicken breast and thigh meat for this recipe.*

# Baked Potato with Spicy Cottage Cheese

*Always choose a variety of potato recommended for baking for this recipe, as the texture of the potato should not be too dry. This makes an excellent low-fat snack any time of the day.*

**SERVES 4**

**INGREDIENTS**
*4 medium baking potatoes*
*225 g/8 oz/1 cup low-fat cottage cheese*
*2 tsp tomato purée (paste)*
*½ tsp ground cumin*
*½ tsp ground coriander*
*½ tsp chilli powder*
*½ tsp salt*
*1 tbsp corn oil*
*½ tsp mixed onion and mustard seeds*
*3 curry leaves*
*2 tbsp water*

**Garnish**
*mixed salad leaves*
*fresh coriander (cilantro) sprigs*
*lemon wedges*
*2 tomatoes, quartered*

I ▲ Preheat the oven to 180°C/350°F/ Gas 4. Wash, pat dry and make a slit in the middle of each potato. Prick the potatoes a few times with a fork, then wrap them individually in foil. Bake in the preheated oven for about 1 hour until soft.

| NUTRITIONAL VALUES (per portion) | |
| --- | --- |
| Total fat | 4.60 g |
| Saturated fat | 0.41 g |
| Cholesterol | 2.81 mg |
| Energy (kcals/kj) | 335/1409 |

**2** Transfer the cottage cheese into a heatproof dish and set aside.

**3** ▲ In a separate bowl, mix together the tomato purée (paste), ground cumin, ground coriander, chilli powder and salt.

**4** ▲ Heat the corn oil in a small saucepan for about 1 minute. Add the mixed onion and mustard seeds and the curry leaves and tilt the saucepan so the oil covers all the seeds and leaves.

**5** When the leaves turn a shade darker and you can smell their beautiful aroma, pour the tomato purée mixture into the saucepan and lower the heat immediately to low. Add the water and mix well.

**6** ▲ Cook for a further 1 minute, then pour the spicy tomato mixture onto the cottage cheese and blend everything together well.

**7** ▲ Check that the potatoes are cooked right through. Unwrap the potatoes and divide the cottage cheese equally between the 4 potatoes.

**8** Garnish with the mixed salad leaves, fresh coriander (cilantro) sprigs, lemon wedges and tomato quarters.

**VARIATION**

*This recipe can also be used as the basis for a tangy vegetable accompaniment to a main meal. Instead of using baked potatoes, boil new potatoes in their skins then cut in half. Add the cooked potatoes to the spicy cottage mixture, mix together well and serve.*

# Tandoori Masala Spring Lamb Chops

*These spicy lean and trimmed lamb chops are marinated for three hours and then cooked in the oven using very little cooking oil. They make an excellent appetizer, served with a salad, and would also serve three as a main course with a rice accompaniment.*

**SERVES 6**

INGREDIENTS
*6 spring lamb chops*
*2 tbsp natural (plain) low-fat yogurt*
*1 tbsp tomato purée (paste)*
*2 tsp ground coriander*
*1 tsp ginger pulp*
*1 tsp garlic pulp*
*1 tsp chilli powder*
*few drops red food colouring (optional)*
*1 tsp salt*
*1 tbsp corn oil*
*3 tbsp lemon juice*
*oil for basting*

**Garnish**
*lettuce leaves (optional)*
*lime wedges*
*1 small onion, sliced*
*fresh coriander (cilantro) sprigs*

**NUTRITIONAL VALUES (per portion)**

| | |
|---|---|
| Total fat | 7.27 g |
| Saturated fat | 2.50 g |
| Cholesterol | 39.70 mg |
| Energy (kcals/kj) | 116/488 |

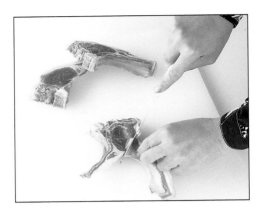

**1 ▲** Rinse the chops and pat dry. Trim off any fat.

**2 ▲** In a medium bowl, mix together the yogurt, tomato purée (paste), ground coriander, ginger, garlic, chilli powder, food colouring, if using, salt, oil and lemon juice.

**3 ▲** Rub this mixture over the chops, using your hands, and leave to marinate for at least 3 hours.

**4 ▲** Preheat the oven to 240°C/475°F/Gas 9. Place the marinated chops in an ovenproof dish.

**5 ▲** Using a brush, baste the chops with about 1 tsp of oil and cook in the preheated oven for 15 minutes. Lower the heat to 180°C/350°F/Gas 4 and cook for a further 10–15 minutes.

**6** Check to see that the chops are cooked and serve immediately on a bed of lettuce leaves, if wished, and garnish with lime wedges, sliced onion and fresh coriander (cilantro) sprigs.

*Opposite: Grazing sheep and their herder*
*Above: Grinding fresh spices in a traditional mortar and pestle*

# Chicken & Meat Dishes

*There are recipes here for every taste and occasion, from Tandoori Chicken and Chicken in a Cashew Nut Sauce, to Spicy Spring Roast Lamb, which makes a wonderful centrepiece for a special meal, and quick-and-easy Lamb with Mint and Peas. By using only lean meat and cooking with the minimal amount of oil, the fat content of all these tasty dishes has been kept to the absolute minimum.*

# Chicken in a Cashew Nut Sauce

*This chicken dish has a delicously thick and nutty sauce, and it is best served with plain boiled rice.*

**SERVES 4**

INGREDIENTS
*2 medium onions*
*2 tbsp tomato purée (paste)*
*50 g/2 oz/¹/₃ cup cashew nuts* √
*1¹/₂ tsp garam masala*
*1 tsp garlic pulp*
*1 tsp chilli powder*
*1 tbsp lemon juice*
*¹/₄ tsp turmeric*
*1 tsp salt*
*1 tbsp natural (plain) low-fat yogurt*
*2 tbsp corn oil*
*1 tbsp chopped fresh coriander (cilantro)*
*1 tbsp sultanas (golden raisins)*
*450 g/1 lb/3¹/₄ cups chicken, skinned, boned and cubed*
*175 g/6 oz/2¹/₂ cups button mushrooms*
*300 ml/¹/₂ pint/1¹/₄ cups water*
*1 tbsp chopped fresh coriander (cilantro)*

| NUTRITIONAL VALUES (per portion) | |
| --- | --- |
| Total fat | 14.64 g |
| Saturated fat | 2.87 g |
| Cholesterol | 64.84 mg |
| Energy (kcals/kj) | 280/1176 |

1 ▲ Cut the onions into quarters and place in a food processor or blender and process for about 1 minute.

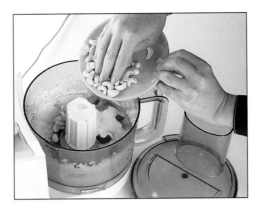

2 ▲ Add the tomato purée (paste), cashew nuts, garam masala, garlic, chilli powder, lemon juice, turmeric, salt and yogurt to the processed onions.

3 Process all the ingredients in the food processor for a further 1–1¹/₂ minutes.

4 In a saucepan, heat the oil, lower the heat to medium and pour in the spice mixture from the food processor. Fry for about 2 minutes, lowering the heat if necessary.

5 ▲ Add the fresh coriander (cilantro), sultanas (golden raisins) and chicken and continue to stir-fry for a further 1 minute.

6 ▲ Add the mushrooms, pour in the water and bring to a simmer. Cover the saucepan and cook over a low heat for about 10 minutes.

7 ▲ After this time, check to see that the chicken is cooked through and the sauce is thick. Cook for a little longer if necessary.

8 Serve garnished with chopped fresh coriander.

# Chicken with Green Mango

*Green, unripe mango is used for making various dishes on the Indian sub-continent, including pickles, chutneys and some meat, chicken and vegetable dishes. This is a fairly simple chicken dish to prepare and is served with rice and dhal.*

**SERVES 4**

### INGREDIENTS

*1 medium green (unripe) mango*
*450 g/1 lb/3¼ cups chicken, skinned, boned and cubed*
*¼ tsp onion seeds*
*1 tsp ginger pulp*
*½ tsp garlic pulp*
*1 tsp chilli powder*
*¼ tsp turmeric*
*1 tsp salt*
*1 tsp ground coriander*
*2 tbsp corn oil*
*2 medium onions, sliced*
*4 curry leaves*
*300 ml/½ pint/1¼ cups water*
*2 medium tomatoes, quartered*
*2 fresh green chillies, chopped*
*2 tbsp chopped fresh coriander (cilantro)*

### NUTRITIONAL VALUES (per portion)

| | |
|---|---|
| Total fat | 11.03 g |
| Saturated fat | 2.43 g |
| Cholesterol | 64.12 mg |
| Energy (kcals/kj) | 269/1131 |

### VARIATION

*A good, firm cooking apple can be used instead of green mango, if wished. Prepare and cook in exactly the same way.*

**1 ▲** To prepare the mango, peel the skin and slice the flesh thickly. Discard the stone (seed) from the middle. Place the mango slices in a small bowl, cover and set aside.

**2 ▲** Place the chicken cubes in a bowl and add the onion seeds, ginger, garlic, chilli powder, turmeric, salt and ground coriander. Mix the spices into the chicken and add half the mango slices to this mixture as well.

**3 ▲** In a medium saucepan, heat the oil and fry the sliced onions until golden brown. Add the curry leaves.

**4 ▲** Gradually add the chicken pieces, stirring all the time.

**5 ▲** Pour in the water, lower the heat and cook for about 12–15 minutes, stirring occasionally, until the chicken is cooked through and the water has been absorbed.

**6 ▲** Add the remaining mango slices, the tomatoes, green chillies and fresh coriander (cilantro) and serve hot.

# Spicy Masala Chicken

*These chicken pieces are grilled (broiled) and have a sweet-and-sour taste. They can be served cold with a salad and rice or hot with Masala Mashed Potatoes.*

**SERVES 6**

INGREDIENTS

12 chicken thighs
6 tbsp lemon juice
1 tsp ginger pulp
1 tsp garlic pulp
1 tsp crushed dried red chillies
1 tsp salt
1 tsp soft brown sugar
2 tbsp clear honey
2 tbsp chopped fresh coriander (cilantro)
1 fresh green chilli, finely chopped
2 tbsp vegetable oil
fresh coriander (cilantro) sprigs

1　Prick the chicken thighs with a fork, rinse, pat dry and set aside in a bowl.

2 ▲ In a large mixing bowl, mix together the lemon juice, ginger, garlic, crushed dried red chillies, salt, sugar and honey.

3　Transfer the chicken thighs to the spice mixture and coat well. Set aside for about 45 minutes.

4 ▲ Preheat the grill (broiler) to medium. Add the fresh coriander (cilantro) and chopped green chilli to the chicken thighs and place them on a flameproof dish.

5 ▲ Pour any remaining marinade over the chicken and baste with the oil, using a pastry brush.

6　Grill (broil) the chicken thighs under the preheated grill for 15–20 minutes, turning and basting occasionally, until cooked through and browned.

7　Transfer to a serving dish and garnish with the fresh coriander sprigs.

# Tandoori Chicken

*A most popular Indian/Pakistan chicken dish which is cooked in a clay oven called a tandoor, this is extremely popular in the West and appears on the majority of the restaurant menus. Though the authentic tandoori flavour is very difficult to achieve in conventional ovens, this version still makes a very tasty dish.*

**SERVES 4**

**INGREDIENTS**
*4 chicken quarters*
*175 ml/6 fl oz/³/4 cup natural (plain) low-fat yogurt*
*1 tsp garam marsala*
*1 tsp ginger pulp*
*1 tsp garlic pulp*
*1¹/2 tsp chilli powder*
*¹/4 tsp turmeric*
*1 tsp ground coriander*
*1 tbsp lemon juice*
*1 tsp salt*
*few drops red food colouring*
*2 tbsp corn oil*

**Garnish**
*mixed salad leaves*
*lime wedges*
*1 tomato, quartered*

**1 ▲** Skin, rinse and pat dry the chicken quarters. Make 2 slits into the flesh of each piece, place in a dish and set aside.

| NUTRITIONAL VALUES (per portion) | |
|---|---|
| Total fat | 10.64 g |
| Saturated fat | 2.74 g |
| Cholesterol | 81.90 mg |
| Energy (kcals/kj) | 242/1018 |

**2 ▲** Mix together the yogurt, garam marsala, ginger, garlic, chilli powder, turmeric, ground coriander, lemon juice, salt, red colouring and oil, and beat so that all the ingredients are well mixed together.

**3** Cover the chicken quarters with the spice mixture and leave to marinate for about 3 hours.

**4 ▲** Preheat the oven to 240°C/475°F/ Gas 9. Transfer the chicken pieces to an ovenproof dish.

**5** Bake in the preheated oven for 20–25 minutes or until the chicken is cooked right through and browned on top.

**6** Remove from the oven, transfer onto a serving dish and garnish with the salad leaves, lime and tomato.

# Hot Chicken Curry

*This curry has a nice thick sauce, and I make it using red and green (bell) peppers for extra colour. It can be served with either Wholemeal (Whole-Wheat) Chapatis or plain boiled rice.*

## SERVES 4

### INGREDIENTS
*2 tbsp corn oil*
*¼ tsp fenugreek seeds*
*¼ tsp onion seeds*
*2 medium onions, chopped*
*½ tsp garlic pulp*
*½ tsp ginger pulp*
*1 tsp ground coriander*
*1 tsp chilli powder*
*1 tsp salt*
*400 g/14 oz/1¾ cups canned tomatoes*
*2 tbsp lemon juice*
*350 g/12 oz/2½ cups chicken, skinned, boned and cubed*
*2 tbsp chopped fresh coriander (cilantro)*
*3 fresh green chillies, chopped*
*½ red (bell) pepper, cut into chunks*
*½ green (bell) pepper, cut into chunks*
*fresh coriander (cilantro) sprigs*

| NUTRITIONAL VALUES (per portion) | |
|---|---|
| Total fat | 9.83 g |
| Saturated fat | 2.03 g |
| Cholesterol | 48.45 mg |
| Energy (kcals/kj) | 205/861 |

1 ▲ In a medium saucepan, heat the oil and fry the fenugreek and onion seeds until they turn a shade darker. Add the chopped onions, garlic and ginger and fry for about 5 minutes until the onions turn golden brown. Lower the heat to very low.

2 ▲ Meanwhile, in a separate bowl, mix together the ground coriander, chilli powder, salt, tomatoes and lemon juice.

3 ▲ Pour this mixture into the saucepan and turn up the heat to medium. Stir-fry for about 3 minutes.

4 ▲ Add the chicken pieces and stir-fry for 5–7 minutes.

5 ▲ Add the fresh coriander (cilantro), green chillies and the sliced (bell) peppers. Lower the heat, cover the saucepan and let this simmer for about 10 minutes until the chicken is cooked.

6 Serve hot, garnished with fresh coriander sprigs.

### COOK'S TIP

*For a milder version of this delicious curry, simply omit some or all of the fresh green chillies.*

# Karahi Chicken with Mint

*For this tasty dish, the chicken is first boiled before being quickly stir-fried in a little oil, to ensure that it is cooked through despite the short cooking time.*

**SERVES 4**

**INGREDIENTS**

275 g/10 oz/2 cups chicken breast fillet,
   skinned and cut into strips
300 ml/½ pint/1¼ cups water
2 tbsp soya oil
2 small bunches spring onions (scallions),
   roughly chopped
1 tsp shredded fresh ginger
1 tsp crushed dried red chilli
2 tbsp lemon juice
1 tbsp chopped fresh coriander (cilantro)
1 tbsp chopped fresh mint
3 tomatoes, seeded and roughly chopped
1 tsp salt
mint and coriander (cilantro) sprigs

| NUTRITIONAL VALUES (per portion) | |
| --- | --- |
| Total fat | 8.20 g |
| Saturated fat | 1.57 g |
| Cholesterol | 30.42 mg |
| Energy (kcals/kj) | 155/649 |

1 ▲ Put the chicken and water into a saucepan, bring to the boil and lower the heat to medium. Cook for about 10 minutes or until the water has evaporated and the chicken is cooked. Remove from the heat and set aside.

2 Heat the oil in a frying pan (skillet) or saucepan and stir-fry the spring onions (scallions) for about 2 minutes until soft.

3 ▲ Add the boiled chicken strips and stir-fry for about 3 minutes over a medium heat.

4 ▲ Gradually add the ginger, dried chilli, lemon juice, fresh coriander (cilantro), fresh mint, tomatoes and salt and gently stir to blend all the flavours together.

5 Transfer to a serving dish and garnish with the fresh mint and coriander sprigs.

# Karahi Chicken with Fresh Fenugreek

*Fresh fenugreek is a flavour that not many people are familiar with and this recipe is a good introduction to this delicious herb.*

## SERVES 4

### INGREDIENTS
*115 g/4 oz/³/4 cup chicken thigh meat, skinned and cut into strips*
*115 g/4 oz/³/4 cup chicken breast fillet, cut into strips*
*¹/2 tsp garlic pulp*
*1 tsp chilli powder*
*¹/2 tsp salt*
*2 tsp tomato purée (paste)*
*2 tbsp soya oil*
*1 bunch fenugreek leaves*
*1 tbsp fresh chopped coriander (cilantro)*
*300 ml/¹/2 pint/1¹/4 cups water*

| NUTRITIONAL VALUES (per portion) | |
| --- | --- |
| Total fat | 8.15 g |
| Saturated fat | 1.64 g |
| Cholesterol | 32.48 mg |
| Energy (kcals/kj) | 128/536 |

**3** Heat the oil in a large saucepan. Lower the heat and add the tomato purée and spice mixture.

**4 ▲** Add the chicken pieces and stir-fry for 5–7 minutes. Lower the heat further.

**5 ▲** Add the fenugreek leaves and fresh coriander (cilantro). Continue to stir-fry for 5–7 minutes.

**6** Pour in the water, cover and cook for about 5 minutes and serve hot with rice or Wholemeal (Whole-Wheat) Chapatis.

## COOK'S TIP

*When preparing fresh fenugreek, use only the leaves and discard the stems which are very bitter in flavour.*

**1 ▲** Bring a saucepan of water to the boil, add the chicken strips and cook for about 5–7 minutes. Drain and set aside.

**2 ▲** In a mixing bowl, combine the garlic, chilli powder and salt with the tomato purée (paste).

# Spicy Spring Lamb Roast

*There are a number of ways of roasting lamb and several different spice mixtures which people use. This is one of my favourite variations.*

**SERVES 6**

INGREDIENTS
*1.5 kg/3 lb leg spring lamb*
*1 tsp chilli powder*
*1 tsp garlic pulp*
*1 tsp ground coriander*
*1 tsp ground cumin*
*1 tsp salt*
*2 tsp desiccated (shredded) coconut*
*2 tsp ground almonds*
*3 tbsp natural (plain) low-fat yogurt*
*2 tbsp lemon juice*
*2 tbsp sultanas (golden raisins)*
*2 tbsp corn oil*

**Garnish**
*mixed salad leaves*
*fresh coriander (cilantro) sprigs*
*2 tomatoes, quartered*
*1 large carrot, cut into julienne strips*
*lemon wedges*

| NUTRITIONAL VALUES (per portion) | |
| --- | --- |
| Total fat | 11.96 g |
| Saturated fat | 4.70 g |
| Cholesterol | 67.38 mg |
| Energy (kcals/kj) | 197/825 |

**1 ▲** Preheat the oven to 180°C/350°F/ Gas 4. Trim off the fat, rinse and pat dry the leg of lamb and set aside on a sheet of foil large enough to enclose the whole joint.

**2 ▲** In a medium bowl, mix together the chilli powder, garlic, ground coriander, ground cumin and salt.

**3 ▲** Grind together in a food processor the desiccated (shredded) coconut, ground almonds, yogurt, lemon juice and sultanas (golden raisins).

**4 ▲** Add the contents of the food processor to the spice mixture together with the corn oil and mix together. Pour this onto the leg of lamb and rub over the meat.

**5** Enclose the meat in the foil and place in an ovenproof dish. Cook in the preheated oven for about 1½ hours.

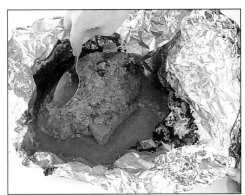

**6 ▲** Remove the lamb from the oven, open the foil and using the back of a spoon spread the mixture evenly over the meat. Return the lamb, uncovered, to the oven for another 45 minutes or until it is cooked right through and is tender.

**7** Slice the meat and serve with the garnish ingredients.

**COOK'S TIP**

*If you don't have any ready-ground almonds to hand, simply process flaked (slivered) or whole blanched almonds in a food processor or coffee grinder.*

# Stuffed Aubergines (Eggplants) with Lamb

*Minced (ground) lamb and aubergines (eggplants) go really well together. This is an attractive dish, using different coloured (bell) peppers in the lightly spiced stuffing mixture.*

**SERVES 4**

## INGREDIENTS
2 medium aubergines (eggplants)
2 tbsp vegetable oil
1 medium onion, sliced
1 tsp ginger pulp
1 tsp chilli powder
1 tsp garlic pulp
1/4 tsp turmeric
1 tsp salt
1 tsp ground coriander
1 medium tomato, chopped
350 g/12 oz lean leg of lamb, minced (ground)
1 medium green (bell) pepper, roughly chopped
1 medium orange (bell) pepper, roughly chopped
2 tbsp chopped fresh coriander (cilantro)

### Garnish
1/2 onion, sliced
2 cherry tomatoes, quartered
fresh coriander (cilantro) sprigs

1  Preheat the oven to 180°C/350°F/Gas 4. Cut the aubergines (eggplants) in half lengthways and scoop out most of the flesh and discard. Place the aubergine shells in a lightly greased ovenproof dish.

| NUTRITIONAL VALUES (per portion) | |
| --- | --- |
| Total fat | 13.92 g |
| Saturated fat | 4.36 g |
| Cholesterol | 67.15 mg |
| Energy (kcals/kj) | 239/1003 |

2  In a medium saucepan, heat 1 tbsp oil and fry the sliced onion until golden brown.

3 ▲ Gradually stir in the ginger, chilli powder, garlic, turmeric, salt and ground coriander. Add the chopped tomato, lower the heat and stir-fry for about 5 minutes.

4 ▲ Add the minced (ground) lamb and continue to stir-fry over a medium heat for 7–10 minutes.

5 ▲ Add the chopped (bell) peppers and fresh coriander (cilantro) to the lamb mixture and stir well.

6 ▲ Spoon the lamb mixture into the aubergine shells and brush the edge of the shells with the remaining oil. Bake in the preheated oven for 20–25 minutes until cooked through and browned on top.

7  Serve with the garnish ingredients and either a green salad or plain boiled rice.

## VARIATION

*For a special occasion, stuffed baby aubergines (eggplants) look particularly attractive. Use 4 small aubergines, leaving the stalks intact, and prepare and cook as described above. Reduce the baking time slightly, if necessary. Large tomatoes or courgettes also make an excellent alternative to aubergines.*

# Lamb with Peas and Mint

*A simple minced (ground) lamb dish, this is easy to prepare and very versatile. It is equally delicious whether served with plain boiled rice or Wholemeal (Whole-Wheat) Chapatis.*

**SERVES 4**

INGREDIENTS
*2 tbsp corn oil*
*1 medium onion, chopped*
*1/2 tsp garlic pulp*
*1/2 tsp ginger pulp*
*1/2 tsp chilli powder*
*1/4 tsp turmeric*
*1 tsp ground coriander*
*1 tsp salt*
*2 medium tomatoes, sliced*
*275 g/10 oz lean leg of lamb, minced (ground)*
*1 large carrot, sliced or cut into batons*
*75 g/3 oz/1/2 cup petit pois*
*1 tbsp chopped fresh mint*
*1 tbsp chopped fresh coriander (cilantro)*
*1 fresh green chilli, chopped*
*coriander (cilantro) sprigs*

| NUTRITIONAL VALUES (per portion) | |
|---|---|
| Total fat | 12.37 g |
| Saturated fat | 3.83 g |
| Cholesterol | 55.89 mg |
| Energy (kcals/kj) | 210/882 |

1 ▲ In a medium saucepan or a deep frying pan (skillet), heat the oil and fry the chopped onions over a medium heat for 5 minutes until golden.

2 ▲ Meanwhile, in a small mixing bowl, blend together the garlic, ginger, chilli powder, turmeric, ground coriander and salt.

3 ▲ When the onions are ready, add the sliced tomatoes and the spice mixture and stir-fry for about 2 minutes.

4 ▲ Add the minced (ground) lamb to the mixture and stir-fry for about 7–10 minutes.

5 ▲ Break up any lumps of meat which may form, using a potato masher if necessary.

6 Finally add the carrot, petit pois, fresh mint, coriander (cilantro) and the fresh green chilli and mix all these together well.

7 Stir-fry for another 2–3 minutes and serve hot, garnished with the coriander sprigs.

# Beef with Green Beans

*Green beans cooked with beef is a variation on the traditional recipe using lamb. The sliced red (bell) pepper used here makes this dish colourful as well as delicious.*

**SERVES 4**

## INGREDIENTS

*275 g/10 oz fine green beans, cut into 2.5 cm/1 in pieces*
*2 tbsp vegetable oil*
*1 medium onion, sliced*
*1 tsp ginger pulp*
*1 tsp garlic pulp*
*1 tsp chilli powder*
*1¼ tsp salt*
*¼ tsp turmeric*
*2 tomatoes, chopped*
*450 g/1 lb beef, cubed*
*1.2 litres/2 pints/5 cups water*
*1 tbsp chopped fresh coriander (cilantro)*
*1 red (bell) pepper, sliced*
*2 fresh green chillies, chopped*

| NUTRITIONAL VALUES (per portion) | |
|---|---|
| Total fat | 11.60 g |
| Saturated fat | 2.89 g |
| Cholesterol | 66.96 mg |
| Energy (kcals/kj) | 241/1011 |

1 ▲ Boil the green beans in salted water for about 5 minutes, then drain and set aside.

2 ▲ Heat the oil in a large saucepan and fry the sliced onion until it turns golden brown.

3 ▲ Mix together the ginger, garlic, chilli powder, salt, turmeric and chopped tomatoes. Spoon this mixture into the onions and stir-fry for 5–7 minutes.

4 Add the beef and stir-fry for a further 3 minutes. Pour in the water, bring to a boil and lower the heat. Cover and cook for 45 minutes to 1 hour until most of the water has evaporated and the meat is tender.

5 ▲ Add the green beans and mix everything together well.

6 ▲ Finally, add the red (bell) pepper, fresh coriander (cilantro) and chopped green chillies and cook, stirring, for a further 7–10 minutes.

7 Serve hot with Wholemeal (Whole-Wheat) Chapatis.

## COOK'S TIP

*Frying onions in very little oil requires some patience. They will take a little longer to brown and should be stirred only occasionally. Excessive stirring will draw the moisture out of the onions and make them even more difficult to fry.*

*Opposite: A fisherman casting his net, Kerala*
*Above: Children fishing with home-made rods*

# Fish & Seafood Dishes

*Fish and seafood, as well as being delicious, are naturally low in fat and cholesterol. These dishes are quick to make, so are perfect for busy cooks with only limited time to spend in the kitchen. They are also very versatile and can be served with accompaniments as a main course, on their own for a nutritious evening meal, or in smaller quantities as appetizers.*

# Fish and Vegetable Kebabs (Kabobs)

*This is a very attractive dish and served on its own will also make an excellent appetizer for eight people.*

**SERVES 4**

INGREDIENTS

*275 g/10 oz cod fillets, or any other firm,
    white fish fillets*
*3 tbsp lemon juice*
*1 tsp ginger pulp*
*2 fresh green chillies, very finely chopped*
*1 tbsp very finely chopped fresh coriander
    (cilantro)*
*1 tbsp very finely chopped fresh mint*
*1 tsp ground coriander*
*1 tsp salt*
*1 red (bell) pepper*
*1 green (bell) pepper*
*½ medium cauliflower*
*8–10 button mushrooms*
*8 cherry tomatoes*
*1 tbsp soya oil*
*1 lime, quartered*

| NUTRITIONAL VALUES (per portion) | |
| --- | --- |
| Total fat | 4.34 g |
| Saturated fat | 0.51 g |
| Cholesterol | 32.54 mg |
| Energy (kcals/kj) | 130/546 |

**1 ▲** Cut the fish fillets into large chunks.

**2 ▲** In a large mixing bowl, blend together the lemon juice, ginger, chopped green chillies, fresh coriander (cilantro), mint, ground coriander and salt. Add the fish chunks and leave to marinate for about 30 minutes.

**3 ▲** Cut the red and green (bell) peppers into large squares and divide the cauliflower into individual florets (flowerets).

**4 ▲** Preheat the grill (broiler) to hot. Arrange the peppers, cauliflower florets, mushrooms and cherry tomatoes alternately with the fish pieces on 4 skewers.

**5 ▲** Baste the kebabs (kabobs) with the oil and any remaining marinade. Transfer to a flameproof dish and grill (broil) under the hot grill for 7–10 minutes or until the fish is cooked right through.

**6** Garnish with the lime quarters, if wished, and serve the kebabs either on their own or with Saffron and Cardamom Flavoured Rice.

**VARIATION**

*Do use different vegetables to the ones suggested, if wished. For example, try baby corn cobs instead of mushrooms and broccoli or one of the new cultivated brassicas in place of the cauliflower.*

# Fish Fillets with a Chilli Sauce

*For this recipe, the fish fillets are first marinated with fresh coriander (cilantro) and lemon juice, then cooked under a hot grill (broiler) and served with a chilli sauce. It is delicious accompanied with Saffron and Cardamom Flavoured Rice.*

**SERVES 4**

## INGREDIENTS

*4 flatfish fillets, such as plaice, sole or*
*    flounder, about 115 g/4 oz each*
*2 tbsp lemon juice*
*1 tbsp finely chopped fresh coriander*
*    (cilantro)*
*1 tbsp vegetable oil*
*lime wedges*
*coriander (cilantro) sprig*

## Sauce

*1 tsp ginger pulp*
*2 tbsp tomato purée (paste)*
*1 tsp sugar*
*1 tsp salt*
*1 tbsp chilli sauce*
*1 tbsp malt vinegar*
*300 ml/1/2 pint/ 1 1/4 cups water*

| NUTRITIONAL VALUES (per portion) | |
|---|---|
| Total fat | 5.28 g |
| Saturated fat | 0.78 g |
| Cholesterol | 47.25 mg |
| Energy (kcals/kj) | 140/586 |

1 ▲ Rinse, pat dry and place the fish fillets in a medium bowl. Add the lemon juice, fresh coriander (cilantro) and oil and rub into the fish. Leave to marinate for at least 1 hour.

2 ▲ Mix together all the sauce ingredients, pour into a small saucepan and simmer over a low heat for about 6 minutes, stirring occasionally.

3  Preheat the grill (broiler) to medium. Place the fillets under the grill for about 5–7 minutes.

4 ▲ When the fillets are cooked, remove and arrange them on a warmed serving dish.

5  The chilli sauce should now be fairly thick – about the consistency of a thick chicken soup.

6 ▲ Pour the sauce over the fillets, garnish with the lime wedges and coriander sprig and serve with rice.

## VARIATION

*For a subtle change in flavour, substitute the lemon juice in the marinade with an equal quantity of lime juice.*

# Grilled (Broiled) Fish Fillets

*The nice thing about fish is that it can be grilled (broiled) beautifully without sacrificing any flavour. For this recipe I have used a minimum amount of oil to baste the fish.*

**SERVES 4**

INGREDIENTS
*4 medium flatfish fillets, such as plaice, sole or flounder, about 115 g/ 4 oz each*
*1 tsp garlic pulp*
*1 tsp garam masala*
*1 tsp chilli powder*
*¼ tsp turmeric*
*½ tsp salt*
*1 tbsp finely chopped fresh coriander (cilantro)*
*1 tbsp vegetable oil*
*2 tbsp lemon juice*

| NUTRITIONAL VALUES (per portion) | |
|---|---|
| Total fat | 5.63 g |
| Saturated fat | 0.84 g |
| Cholesterol | 47.25 mg |
| Energy (kcals/kj) | 143/599 |

1 ▲ Line a flameproof dish or grill (broiler) tray with foil. Rinse and pat dry the fish fillets and put them on the foil-lined dish or tray.

2 ▲ In a small bowl, mix together the garlic, garam masala, chilli powder, turmeric, salt, fresh coriander (cilantro), oil and lemon juice.

3 ▲ Using a pastry brush, baste the fish fillets evenly all over with the spice and lemon juice mixture.

4 Preheat the grill to very hot, then lower the heat to medium. Grill (broil) the fillets for about 10 minutes, basting occasionally, until they are cooked right through.

5 Serve immediately with an attractive garnish, such as grated carrot, tomato quarters and lime slices, if wished.

# Glazed Garlic Prawns (Shrimp)

*A fairly simple and quick dish to prepare, it is best to peel the prawns (shrimp) as this helps them to absorb maximum flavour. Serve as a main course with accompaniments, or with a salad as an appetizer.*

**SERVES 4**

### INGREDIENTS

*1 tbsp vegetable oil*
*3 garlic cloves, roughly chopped*
*3 tomatoes, chopped*
*½ tsp salt*
*1 tsp crushed dried red chillies*
*1 tsp lemon juice*
*1 tbsp mango chutney*
*1 fresh green chilli, chopped*
*15–20 cooked king prawns (jumbo shrimp), peeled*
*fresh coriander (cilantro) sprigs*
*2 spring onions (scallions), chopped (optional)*

### NUTRITIONAL VALUES (per portion)

| | |
|---|---|
| Total fat | 3.83 g |
| Saturated fat | 0.54 g |
| Cholesterol | 30.37 mg |
| Energy (kcals/kj) | 90/380 |

1 ▲ In a medium saucepan, heat the oil and add the chopped garlic.

2 ▲ Lower the heat and add the chopped tomatoes along with the salt, crushed chillies, lemon juice, mango chutney and chopped fresh chilli.

3 ▲ Finally add the prawns (shrimp), turn up the heat and stir-fry these quickly, until heated through.

4 Transfer to a serving dish. Serve garnished with fresh coriander (cilantro) sprigs and chopped spring onions (scallions), if wished.

# Prawn (Shrimp) and Spinach Pancakes (Crêpes)

*Serve these delicious filled pancakes (crêpes) hot with the Spicy Baby Vegetable Salad. Try to use red onions for this recipe, although they are not essential.*

**MAKES 4–6 PANCAKES (CRÊPES)**

### INGREDIENTS
**Pancakes (Crêpes)**
*175 g/6 oz/1½ cups plain (all-purpose) flour*
*½ tsp salt*
*3 eggs*
*1½ cups semi-skimmed (2%) milk*
*15 g/½ oz/1 tbsp low-fat margarine*

**Filling**
*2 tbsp vegetable oil*
*2 medium red onions, sliced*
*½ tsp garlic pulp*
*2.5 cm/1 in piece ginger, shredded*
*1 tsp chilli powder*
*1 tsp garam masala*
*1 tsp salt*
*2 tomatoes, sliced*
*225 g/8 oz frozen leaf spinach, thawed and drained*
*115 g/4 oz cooked prawns (shrimp)*
*2 tbsp chopped fresh coriander (cilantro)*

**Garnish**
*1 tomato, quartered*
*fresh coriander (cilantro) sprigs*
*lemon wedges*

### NUTRITIONAL VALUES (per portion)

| | |
|---|---|
| Total fat | 14.04 g |
| Saturated fat | 3.19 g |
| Cholesterol | 173.33 mg |
| Energy (kcals/kj) | 373/1568 |

1 ▲ To make the pancakes (crêpes), sift the flour and salt together. Beat the eggs and add to the flour, beating continuously. Gradually stir in the milk. Leave to stand for 1 hour.

2 Heat the oil in a deep frying pan (skillet) and fry the sliced onions over a medium heat until golden.

3 ▲ Gradually add the garlic, ginger, chilli powder, garam masala and salt, followed by the tomatoes and spinach, stir-frying constantly.

4 ▲ Add the prawns (shrimp) and fresh coriander (cilantro). Cook for a further 5–7 minutes or until any excess water has been absorbed. Keep warm.

5 ▲ Heat about ½ tsp of the low-fat margarine in a 25 cm/10 in non-stick frying pan (skillet) or pancake pan. Pour in about one-quarter of the pancake batter, tilting the pan so the batter spreads well, coats the bottom of the pan and is evenly distributed.

6 ▲ When fine bubbles begin to appear on top, flip it over using a spatula and cook for a further minute or so. Transfer to a plate and keep warm. Cook the remaining pancakes in the same way.

7 Fill the pancakes with the spinach and prawns and garnish with the tomato and fresh coriander sprigs. Serve warm with lemon wedges.

# Prawns (Shrimp) with Vegetables

*This is a light and nutritious dish, excellent served either on a bed of lettuce leaves, with plain boiled rice or Wholemeal (Whole-Wheat) Chapatis.*

**SERVES 4**

INGREDIENTS

*2 tbsp chopped fresh coriander (cilantro)*
*1 tsp salt*
*2 fresh green chillies, seeded if wished*
*3 tbsp lemon juice*
*2 tbsp vegetable oil*
*20 cooked king prawns (jumbo shrimp), peeled*
*1 medium courgette (zucchini), thickly sliced*
*1 medium onion, cut into 8 chunks*
*8 cherry tomatoes*
*8 baby corn cobs*
*mixed salad leaves*

| **NUTRITIONAL VALUES (per portion)** | |
| --- | --- |
| Total fat | 6.47 g |
| Saturated fat | 0.85 g |
| Cholesterol | 29.16 mg |
| Energy (kcals/kj) | 109/458 |

**1 ▲** Place the chopped coriander (cilantro), salt, green chillies, lemon juice and oil in a food processor and grind these together for a few seconds.

**2 ▲** Remove the contents from the processor and transfer to a medium mixing bowl.

**3 ▲** Add the peeled prawns (shrimp) to this mixture and stir to make sure that all the prawns are well coated. Set aside to marinate for about 30 minutes.

**4** Preheat the grill (broiler) to very hot, then turn the heat down to medium.

**5 ▲** Arrange the vegetables and prawns alternately on 4 skewers. When all the skewers are ready place them under the preheated grill for 5–7 minutes until cooked and browned.

**6** Serve immediately on a bed of mixed salad leaves.

**COOK'S TIP**

*King prawns (jumbo shrimp) are a luxury, but worth choosing for a special dinner. For a more economical variation, substitute the king prawns with 450 g/1 lb ordinary prawns.*

*Opposite and above: An abundance of fresh vegetables on offer at road-side stalls and markets*

# Vegetable Dishes

*Everyone should eat fresh vegetables regularly for good health, and with the ever-increasing range of produce now available all year round there is no excuse for not serving a vegetable accompaniment with all your meals. These delicately spiced recipes will complement any of the main course dishes in this book, or try Potatoes with Red Chillies or Masala Beans with Fenugreek with simply grilled (broiled) chicken or fish.*

# Okra in Yogurt

*This tangy vegetable dish can be served as an accompaniment, but also makes an excellent vegetarian meal served with Tarka Dhal and Wholemeal (Whole-Wheat) Chapatis.*

## SERVES 4

INGREDIENTS
*450 g/1 lb okra*
*2 tbsp corn oil*
*½ tsp onion seeds*
*3 medium fresh green chillies, chopped*
*1 medium onion, sliced*
*¼ tsp turmeric*
*2 tsp desiccated (shredded) coconut*
*½ tsp salt*
*1 tbsp natural (plain) low-fat yogurt*
*2 medium tomatoes, sliced*
*1 tbsp chopped fresh coriander (cilantro)*

### NUTRITIONAL VALUES (per portion)

| | |
|---|---|
| Total fat | 8.44 g |
| Saturated fat | 2.09 g |
| Cholesterol | 0.15 mg |
| Energy (kcals/kj) | 119/501 |

1 ▲ Wash, top and tail the okra, cut into 1 cm/½ in pieces and set aside.

2 ▲ Heat the oil in a medium frying pan (skillet), add the onion seeds, green chillies and onion and fry for about 5 minutes until the onion has turned golden brown.

3 ▲ Lower the heat and add the turmeric, desiccated (shredded) coconut and salt and fry for about 1 minute.

4 ▲ Next add the okra, turn the heat to medium-high and quickly stir-fry for a few minutes until lightly golden.

5 ▲ Add the yogurt, tomatoes and finally the fresh coriander (cilantro). Cook for a further 2 minutes.

6 Transfer onto a serving dish and serve immediately.

# Courgettes (Zucchini) with Mushrooms in a Creamy Sauce

*When cream and mushrooms are cooked together they complement each other beautifully. Though this dish sounds very rich, by using single (light) cream and very little oil you can keep the fat content to a minimum.*

**SERVES 4**

**INGREDIENTS**
*2 tbsp vegetable oil*
*1 medium onion, roughly chopped*
*1 tsp ground coriander*
*1 tsp ground cumin*
*1 tsp salt*
*1/2 tsp chilli powder*
*225 g/8 oz/3 cups mushrooms, sliced*
*2 medium courgettes (zucchini), sliced*
*3 tbsp single (light) cream*
*1 tbsp chopped fresh coriander (cilantro)*

| NUTRITIONAL VALUES (per portion) | |
| --- | --- |
| Total fat | 7.73 g |
| Saturated fat | 1.80 g |
| Cholesterol | 4.50 mg |
| Energy (kcals/kj) | 95/400 |

1 ▲ Heat the oil and fry the chopped onions until golden brown. Lower the heat to medium, add the ground coriander, cumin, salt and chilli powder and stir together well.

2 ▲ Once the onions and the spices are well blended, add the mushrooms and courgettes (zucchini) and stir-fry gently for about 5 minutes until soft. If the mixture is too dry just add a little water to loosen.

3 ▲ Finally pour in the cream and mix it well into the vegetables.

4 Garnish with fresh chopped coriander (cilantro), if wished, and serve immediately.

# Potatoes with Red Chillies

*The quantity of red chillies used here may be too fiery for some palates. For a milder version, either seed the chillies, use fewer or substitute them with 1 roughly chopped red (bell) pepper.*

**SERVES 4**

INGREDIENTS

*12–14 baby new potatoes, peeled and halved*
*2 tbsp vegetable oil*
*1/2 tsp crushed dried red chillies*
*1/2 tsp white cumin seeds*
*1/2 tsp fennel seeds*
*1/2 tsp crushed coriander seeds*
*1 tbsp salt*
*1 medium onion, sliced*
*1–4 fresh red chillies, chopped*
*1 tbsp chopped fresh coriander (cilantro)*

| NUTRITIONAL VALUES (per portion) | |
|---|---|
| Total fat | 6.31 g |
| Saturated fat | 0.75 g |
| Cholesterol | 0.00 mg |
| Energy (kcals/kj) | 151/634 |

**2 ▲** In a deep frying pan (skillet), heat the oil, then turn down the heat to medium. Then add the crushed chillies, cumin, fennel and coriander seeds and salt and fry for 30–40 seconds.

**3 ▼** Add the sliced onion and fry until golden brown. Then add the potatoes, red chillies and fresh coriander (cilantro).

**4** Cover and cook for 5–7 minutes over a very low heat. Serve hot.

**1 ▲** Boil the baby potatoes in salted water until soft but still firm. Remove from the heat and drain off the water.

# Potatoes in a Yogurt Sauce

*It is nice to use tiny new potatoes with the skins on for this recipe. The yogurt adds a tangy flavour to this fairly spicy dish, which is delicious served with Wholemeal (Whole-Wheat) Chapatis.*

## SERVES 4

### INGREDIENTS

*12 new potatoes, halved*
*275 g/10 oz/1¼ cups natural (plain) low-fat yogurt*
*300 ml/½ pint/1¼ cups water*
*¼ tsp turmeric*
*1 tsp chilli powder*
*1 tsp ground coriander*
*½ tsp ground cumin*
*1 tsp salt*
*1 tsp soft brown sugar*
*2 tbsp vegetable oil*
*1 tsp white cumin seeds*
*1 tbsp chopped fresh coriander (cilantro)*
*2 fresh green chillies, sliced*
*1 fresh coriander sprig (optional)*

### NUTRITIONAL VALUES (per portion)

| | |
|---|---|
| Total fat | 6.84 g |
| Saturated fat | 1.11 g |
| Cholesterol | 2.80 mg |
| Energy (kcals/kj) | 184/774 |

1 ▲ Boil the potatoes in salted water with their skins on until they are just tender, then drain and set aside.

2 ▲ Mix together the yogurt, water, turmeric, chilli powder, ground coriander, ground cumin, salt and sugar in a bowl. Set aside.

3 ▲ Heat the oil in a medium saucepan and add the white cumin seeds.

4 ▲ Reduce the heat, stir in the yogurt mixture and cook for about 3 minutes over a medium heat.

5 ▲ Add the fresh coriander (cilantro), green chillies and cooked potatoes. Blend everything together and cook for a further 5–7 minutes, stirring occasionally.

6 Transfer to a serving dish and garnish with the coriander sprig, if wished.

### COOK'S TIP

*If new potatoes are unavailable, use 450 g/2 lb ordinary potatoes instead. Peel them and cut into large chunks, then cook as described above.*

# Masala Mashed Potatoes

*These potatoes are very versatile and will perk up any meal.*

**SERVES 4**

**INGREDIENTS**
*3 medium potatoes*
*1 tbsp chopped fresh mint and coriander*
   *(cilantro), mixed*
*1 tsp mango powder*
*1 tsp salt*
*1 tsp crushed black peppercorns*
*1 fresh red chilli, chopped*
*1 fresh green chilli, chopped*
*50 g/2 oz/4 tbsp low-fat margarine*

| NUTRITIONAL VALUES (per portion) | |
| --- | --- |
| Total fat | 5.80 g |
| Saturated fat | 1.25 g |
| Cholesterol | 0.84 mg |
| Energy (kcals/kj) | 94/394 |

I  Boil the potatoes until soft enough to be mashed. Mash these down using a masher.

2 ▲ Blend together the remaining ingredients in a small bowl.

3 ▲ Stir the mixture into the mashed potatoes and mix together thoroughly with a fork.

4  Serve warm as an accompaniment.

# Spicy Cabbage

*An excellent vegetable accompaniment, this is very versatile and can be served even as a warm side salad.*

**SERVES 4**

**INGREDIENTS**
*50 g/2 oz/4 tbsp low-fat margarine*
*1/2 tsp white cumin seeds*
*3–8 dried red chillies, to taste*
*1 small onion, sliced*
*225 g/8 oz/2 1/2 cups cabbage, shredded*
*2 medium carrots, grated*
*1/2 tsp salt*
*2 tbsp lemon juice*

| NUTRITIONAL VALUES (per portion) | |
| --- | --- |
| Total fat | 6.06 g |
| Saturated fat | 1.28 g |
| Cholesterol | 0.84 mg |
| Energy (kcals/kj) | 92/384 |

2 ▲ Add the sliced onion and fry for about 2 minutes. Add the cabbage and carrots and stir-fry for a further 5 minutes or until the cabbage is soft.

3  Finally, stir in the salt and lemon juice and serve.

I ▲ Melt the low-fat margarine in a medium saucepan and fry the white cumin seeds and dried red chillies for about 30 seconds.

*Masala Mashed Potatoes (top) and Spicy Cabbage*

# Masala Beans with Fenugreek

*"Masala" means spice and this vegetarian dish is spicy, though not necessarily hot.*

**SERVES 4**

## INGREDIENTS

*1 medium onion*
*1 tsp ground cumin*
*1 tsp ground coriander*
*1 tsp sesame seeds*
*1 tsp chilli powder*
*¹/₂ tsp garlic pulp*
*¹/₄ tsp turmeric*
*1 tsp salt*
*2 tbsp vegetable oil*
*1 tomato, quartered*
*225 g/8 oz French (green) beans*
*1 bunch fresh fenugreek leaves, stems discarded*
*4 tbsp chopped fresh coriander (cilantro)*
*1 tbsp lemon juice*

| NUTRITIONAL VALUES (per portion) | |
| --- | --- |
| Total fat | 7.11 g |
| Saturated fat | 0.88 g |
| Cholesterol | 0.00 mg |
| Energy (kcals/kj) | 100/419 |

1  Roughly chop the onion. Mix together the ground cumin and coriander, sesame seeds, chilli powder, garlic, turmeric and salt.

2 ▲ Place all of these ingredients, including the onion, in a food processor and process for 30–45 seconds.

3 ▲ In a medium saucepan, heat the oil and fry the spice mixture for about 5 minutes, stirring occasionally.

4 ▲ Add the tomato, French (green) beans, fresh fenugreek and fresh coriander (cilantro).

5 ▲ Stir-fry for about 5 minutes, sprinkle in the lemon juice and serve.

# Vegetables with Almonds

*Natural (plain) yogurt is added to the vegetables towards the end of the cooking time, which not only gives this dish a tangy note but also makes it creamy.*

**SERVES 4**

INGREDIENTS
2 tbsp vegetable oil
2 medium onions, sliced
5 cm/2 in piece fresh ginger, shredded
1 tsp crushed black peppercorns
1 bay leaf
¼ tsp turmeric
1 tsp ground coriander
1 tsp salt
½ tsp garam masala
175 g/6 oz/2½ cups mushrooms, thickly
    sliced
1 medium courgette (zucchini), thickly
    sliced
50 g/2 oz French beans, sliced into
    2.5 cm/1 in pieces
1 tbsp roughly chopped fresh mint
150 ml/¼ pint/⅔ cup water
2 tbsp natural (plain) low-fat yogurt
25 g/1 oz/¼ cup flaked (slivered) almonds

| NUTRITIONAL VALUES (per portion) | |
|---|---|
| Total fat | 10.11 g |
| Saturated fat | 1.14 g |
| Cholesterol | 0.30 mg |
| Energy (kcals/kj) | 136/569 |

**2 ▲** Lower the heat and add the turmeric, ground coriander, salt and garam masala, stirring occasionally. Gradually add the mushrooms, courgette (zucchini), French beans and the mint. Stir gently so that the vegetables retain their shapes.

**3** Pour in the water and bring to a simmer, then lower the heat and cook until the water has been absorbed by the vegetables.

**4 ▲** Beat the yogurt with a fork, then pour onto the vegetables and mix together well.

**5** Cook for a further 2–3 minutes, stirring occasionally. Serve garnished with the flaked (slivered) almonds.

**1 ▲** In a medium deep frying pan (skillet), heat the oil and fry the sliced onions with the shredded ginger, crushed black peppercorns and bay leaf for 3–5 minutes.

# Sweet-and-Sour Vegetables with Paneer

*This is one of my favourite grilled (broiled) vegetable selections. The cheese used in this recipe is Indian paneer, which can be bought at some Asian stores; tofu can be used in its place.*

**SERVES 4**

INGREDIENTS

*1 green pepper, cut into squares*
*1 yellow pepper, cut into squares*
*8 cherry, or 4 salad, tomatoes*
*8 cauliflower florets (flowerets)*
*8 pineapple chunks*
*8 cubes paneer (see Introduction)*

**Seasoned oil**

*1 tbsp soya oil*
*2 tbsp lemon juice*
*1 tsp salt*
*1 tsp crushed black peppercorns*
*1 tbsp clear honey*
*2 tbsp chilli sauce*

**NUTRITIONAL VALUES (per portion)**

| | |
|---|---|
| Total fat | 9.80 g |
| Saturated fat | 4.43 g |
| Cholesterol | 20.00 mg |
| Energy (kcals/kj) | 171/718 |

1 ▲ Preheat the grill (broiler) to hot. Thread the prepared vegetables, pineapple and the paneer onto 4 skewers, alternating the ingredients. Set the skewers on a flameproof dish or grill tray.

2 In a small mixing bowl, mix all the ingredients for the seasoned oil. If the mixture is a little too thick, add 1 tbsp of water to loosen it.

3 ▲ Using a pastry brush, baste the vegetables with the seasoned oil. Grill (broil) under the preheated grill for about 10 minutes until the vegetables begin to darken slightly, turning the skewers to cook evenly.

4 Serve on a bed of plain boiled rice.

# Vegetables and Beans with Curry Leaves

*Fresh curry leaves are extremely aromatic and there is no substitute for them. Fresh curry leaves also freeze well, but if necessary you can use dried ones. This is quite a dry curry.*

**SERVES 4**

INGREDIENTS

*2 tbsp vegetable oil*
*6 curry leaves*
*3 garlic cloves, sliced*
*3 dried red chillies*
*1/4 tsp onion seeds*
*1/4 tsp fenugreek seeds*
*3 fresh green chillies, chopped*
*2 tsp desiccated (shredded) coconut*
*115 g/4 oz/1/2 cup canned red kidney beans, drained*

*1 medium carrot, cut into strips*
*50 g/2 oz French beans, diagonally sliced*
*1 medium red (bell) pepper, cut into strips*
*1 tsp salt*
*2 tbsp lemon juice*

**NUTRITIONAL VALUES (per portion)**

| | |
|---|---|
| Total fat | 8.27 g |
| Saturated fat | 2.47 g |
| Cholesterol | 0.00 mg |
| Energy (kcals/kj) | 130/548 |

1 Heat the oil in a medium deep frying pan (skillet). Add the curry leaves, garlic cloves, dried chillies, and onion and fenugreek seeds.

2 ▲ When these turn a shade darker, add the remaining ingredients, stirring constantly. Lower the heat, cover and cook for about 5 minutes.

3 Transfer to a serving dish and serve with extra coconut, if wished.

*Sweet-and-Sour Vegetables with Paneer (top) and Vegetables and Beans with Curry Leaves*

*Opposite and above: Woman working in the fields, gathering and tending crops*

# Breads, Rice & Lentil Dishes

*Indian meals are not considered complete without a bread or rice accompaniment. Plain boiled basmati rice is the most popular way to serve rice, but try aromatic Saffron and Cardamom Flavoured Rice or Pea and Mushroom Pullao for special occasions. Wholemeal (Whole-Wheat) Chapatis are the ideal low-fat accompaniment for any Indian meal, and a low-fat version of Tarka Dhal, a spicy lentil dish, is delicious served with curries that are rather dry in texture.*

# Saffron and Cardamom Flavoured Rice

*There are two main ways of cooking rice: one is total absorption of water and the other is where you drain the water, which gets rid of any starch from the rice. For this recipe I have chosen the latter for obvious reasons.*

**SERVES 6**

## INGREDIENTS
*450 g/1 lb/2¼ cups basmati rice*
*750 ml/1¼ pints/good 3 cups water*
*3 green cardamom pods*
*2 cloves*
*1 tsp salt*
*½ tsp crushed saffron strands*
*3 tbsp semi-skimmed (2%) milk*

| NUTRITIONAL VALUES (per portion) | |
|---|---|
| Total fat | 0.79 g |
| Saturated fat | 0.19 g |
| Cholesterol | 1.31 mg |
| Energy (kcals/kj) | 264/1108 |

1 ▲ Wash the rice at least twice and place it in a medium saucepan with the water.

2 ▲ Toss all the whole spices into the saucepan along with the salt. Bring to the boil, cover and simmer for about 10 minutes.

3 Meanwhile, place the saffron and semi-skimmed (2%) milk in a small pan and warm. Alternatively, put the ingredients in a cup and warm for 1 minute in the microwave.

4 ▲ Now return to the rice to see if it is fully cooked. Use a slotted spoon to lift out a few grains and press the rice between your index finger and thumb. It should feel soft on the outside but still a little hard in the middle.

5 Remove the pan from the heat and carefully drain the rice through a sieve (strainer).

6 ▲ Transfer the rice back into the pan and pour the saffron and milk over the top of the rice.

7 ▲ Cover with a tight-fitting lid and place the pan back on a medium heat for 7–10 minutes.

8 After cooking, remove the pan from the heat and leave the rice to stand for a further 5 minutes before serving.

## COOK'S TIP

*Basmati rice is unequalled in flavour and texture and is the best variety to choose for Indian rice dishes. It is available from large supermarkets and Asian stores.*

# Tomato Rice

*This is delicious and can be eaten as a complete meal on its own.*

**SERVES 4**

**INGREDIENTS**
*2 tbsp corn oil*
*½ tsp onion seeds*
*1 medium onion, sliced*
*2 medium tomatoes, sliced*
*1 orange or yellow (bell) pepper, sliced*
*1 tsp ginger pulp*
*1 tsp garlic pulp*
*1 tsp chilli powder*
*2 tbsp chopped fresh coriander (cilantro)*
*1 medium potato, diced*
*1½ tsp salt*
*50 g/2 oz/⅓ cup frozen peas*
*400 g/14 oz/2 cups basmati rice, washed*
*700 ml/24 fl oz/3 cups water*

| NUTRITIONAL VALUES (per portion) | |
| --- | --- |
| Total fat | 6.48 g |
| Saturated fat | 0.86 g |
| Cholesterol | 0.00 mg |
| Energy (kcals/kj) | 351/1475 |

I ▲ Heat the oil and fry the onion seeds for about 30 seconds. Add the sliced onion and fry for about 5 minutes.

2 ▲ Start adding the sliced tomatoes, (bell) pepper, ginger, garlic, chilli powder, fresh coriander (cilantro), potatoes, salt and peas and stir-fry over a medium heat for a further 5 minutes.

3 Add the rice and stir for about 1 minute.

4 Pour in the water and bring to the boil, then lower the heat to medium. Cover and cook for 12–15 minutes. Leave the rice to stand for 5 minutes and then serve.

# Pea and Mushroom Pullao

*It is best to use button mushrooms and petit pois for this delectable rice dish as they make the pullao look truly attractive and appetizing.*

**SERVES 6**

**INGREDIENTS**
*2 tbsp vegetable oil*
*½ tsp black cumin seeds*
*2 black cardamom pods*
*2 cinnamon sticks*
*3 garlic cloves, sliced*
*1 tsp salt*
*1 medium tomato, sliced*
*50 g/2 oz/⅔ cup button mushrooms*
*450 g/1 lb/2¼ cups basmati rice*
*75 g/3 oz/heaped ⅓ cup petit pois*
*750 ml/1¼ pints/good 3 cups water*

| NUTRITIONAL VALUES (per portion) | |
| --- | --- |
| Total fat | 4.34 g |
| Saturated fat | 0.49 g |
| Cholesterol | 0.00 mg |
| Energy (kcals/kj) | 297/1246 |

I Wash the rice at least twice and set aside in a sieve (strainer).

2 ▲ In a medium saucepan, heat the oil and add the spices, garlic and salt.

3 ▲ Add the sliced tomato and button mushrooms and stir-fry for 2–3 minutes.

4 Now add the rice and peas and gently stir around, making sure you do not break the rice.

5 Add the water and bring the mixture to the boil. Lower the heat, cover and continue to cook for 15–20 minutes.

*Tomato Rice (top) and Pea and Mushroom Pullao*

# Chicken Pullao

*This dish is a complete meal on its own, but is also delicious served with a lentil dish such as Tarka Dhal.*

**SERVES 4**

**INGREDIENTS**
*75 g/3 oz/6 tbsp low-fat margarine*
*1 medium onion, sliced*
*1/4 tsp mixed onion and mustard seeds*
*3 curry leaves*
*1 tsp ginger pulp*
*1 tsp garlic pulp*
*1 tsp ground coriander*
*1 tsp chilli powder*
*1 1/2 tsp salt*
*2 tomatoes, sliced*
*1 medium potato, cubed*
*50 g/2 oz/1/3 cup frozen peas*
*175 g/6 oz/1 1/4 cups chicken, skinned, boned and cubed*
*400 g/14 oz/2 cups basmati rice*
*4 tbsp chopped fresh coriander (cilantro)*
*2 fresh green chillies, chopped*
*700 ml/24 fl oz/3 cups water*

| NUTRITIONAL VALUES (per portion) | |
| --- | --- |
| Total fat | 8.50 g |
| Saturated fat | 1.96 g |
| Cholesterol | 25.06 mg |
| Energy (kcals/kj) | 406/1707 |

1  Wash and soak the rice for 30 minutes, then set aside in a sieve (strainer).

**2 ▲** In a medium saucepan, melt the low-fat margarine and fry the sliced onion until golden.

**3 ▲** Add the onion and mustard seeds, the curry leaves, ginger, garlic, ground coriander, chilli powder and salt. Stir-fry for about 2 minutes.

**4 ▲** Add the sliced tomatoes, cubed potato, peas and chicken and mix everything together well.

**5 ▲** Add the rice and stir gently to combine with the other ingredients.

**6 ▲** Finally, add the fresh coriander (cilantro) and chopped green chillies. Mix and stir-fry for a further 1 minute. Pour in the water.

**7**  Bring to the boil and lower the heat. Cover and cook for about 20 minutes.

# Tarka Dhal

*Tarka dhal is probably the most popular of lentil dishes and is found in most Indian/Pakistani restaurants.*

**SERVES 4**

INGREDIENTS

*115 g/4 oz/¹/₂ cup masoor dhal (split red lentils)*
*50 g/2 oz/¹/₄ cup moong dhal (small split yellow lentils)*
*600 ml/1 pint/2¹/₂ cups water*
*1 tsp ginger pulp*
*1 tsp garlic pulp*
*¹/₄ tsp turmeric*
*2 fresh green chillies, chopped*
*1¹/₂ tsp salt*

**Tarka**

*2 tbsp vegetable oil*
*1 onion, sliced*
*¹/₄ tsp mixed mustard and onion seeds*
*4 dried red chillies*
*1 tomato, sliced*

**Garnish**

*1 tbsp chopped fresh coriander (cilantro)*
*1–2 fresh green chillies, seeded and sliced*
*1 tbsp chopped fresh mint*

| NUTRITIONAL VALUES (per portion) | |
|---|---|
| Total fat | 6.61 g |
| Saturated fat | 0.90 g |
| Cholesterol | 0.00 mg |
| Energy (kcals/kj) | 179/752 |

1 Pick over the lentils for any stones before washing them.

2 ▲ Boil the lentils in the water with the ginger, garlic, turmeric and chopped green chillies for 15–20 minutes or until soft.

3 ▲ Mash the lentil mixture down. The consistency of the mashed lentils should be similar to a creamy chicken soup.

4 ▲ If the mixture looks too dry, add more water. Season with the salt.

5 ▲ To prepare the tarka, heat the oil and fry the onion with the mustard and onion seeds, dried red chillies and sliced tomato for 2 minutes.

6 ▲ Pour the tarka over the dhal and garnish with fresh coriander (cilantro), green chillies and mint.

**COOK'S TIP**

*Dried red chillies are available in many different sizes. If the ones you have are large, or if you want a less spicy flavour, reduce the quantity specified to 1–2.*

# Naan

*There are various recipes for making naan, but this one is particularly easy to follow. Always serve naan warm, preferably straight from the grill (broiler), or wrap them in foil until you are ready to serve the meal.*

**NUTRITIONAL VALUES** (per portion)

| | |
|---|---|
| Total fat | 5.07 g |
| Saturated fat | 1.24 g |
| Cholesterol | 0.50 mg |
| Energy (kcals/kj) | 177/744 |

**MAKES 6**

INGREDIENTS

*1 tsp caster (superfine) sugar*
*1 tsp dried (active dry) yeast*
*150 ml/¼ pint/⅔ cup warm water*
*225 g/8 oz/2 cups plain (all-purpose) flour*
*1 tsp ghee, or butter*
*1 tsp salt*
*50 g/2 oz/¼ cup low-fat margarine, melted*
*1 tsp poppy seeds*

1  Put the sugar and yeast in a small bowl, add the warm water and mix well until the yeast has dissolved. Leave on one side for 10 minutes or until the mixture becomes frothy.

2 ▲ Place the flour in a large mixing bowl, make a well in the middle and add the ghee, or butter, and salt, then pour in the yeast mixture.

3 ▲ Mix well, using your hands, to make a dough, adding some more water if the dough is too dry. Turn out onto a floured surface and knead for about 5 minutes or until smooth.

4 ▲ Place the dough back in the bowl, cover with foil and leave to rise in a warm place for 1½ hours or until doubled in size.

5 ▲ Preheat the grill (broiler) to very hot. Turn out the dough onto a floured surface and knead for a further 2 minutes. Break off small balls with your hand and roll into circles or ovals about 12 cm (5 in) in diameter and 1 cm (½ in) thick.

6  Place on a sheet of greased foil and grill (broil) for 7–10 minutes, turning twice to brush with butter and sprinkle with poppy seeds.

# Wholemeal (Whole-Wheat) Chapatis

*This is one of the less-fattening Indian breads as it contains no fat. Some cooks like to brush the chapati with a little melted butter before serving. Ideally the chapatis should be eaten as soon as they come off the tava (chapati griddle) or frying pan (skillet), but if that is not practical keep them warm wrapped in foil. Allow two per person.*

**MAKES 8–10**

**INGREDIENTS**
*225 g/8 oz/2 cups wholemeal (whole-wheat) flour*
*1/2 tsp salt*
*175 ml/6 fl oz/3/4 cup water*

| NUTRITIONAL VALUES (per portion) | |
|---|---|
| Total fat | 0.62 g |
| Saturated fat | 0.08 g |
| Cholesterol | 0.00 mg |
| Energy (kcals/kj) | 87/366 |

I ▲ Place the flour and salt in a mixing bowl. Make a well in the middle and gradually stir in the water, mixing well with your fingers.

2 ▲ Form a supple dough and knead for 7–10 minutes. Ideally, cover with clear film (plastic wrap) and leave on one side for 15–20 minutes. If time is short roll out straight away.

3 ▲ Divide the dough into 8–10 equal portions. Roll out each piece in a circle on a well-floured surface.

4 Place a tava or heavy-based frying pan (skillet) over a high heat. When steam rises from it, lower the heat to medium and add the first chapati to the pan.

5 ▲ When the chapati begins to bubble, turn it over. Press down with a clean dish towel or a flat spoon and turn once again. Remove from the pan and keep warm in foil.

6 Repeat the process until all the chapatis are cooked.

*Opposite: The busy market on Morning Street, Dehli*
*Above: A road-side salad stall, Dehli*

# Salads

*Salads are an excellent choice as side dishes for anyone following a strict diet — and the ones chosen here will be enjoyed by everyone. Instead of the simple mixed green variety, ring the changes and try Spinach and Mushroom Salad or Spicy Baby Vegetable Salad. Sweet Potato and Carrot Salad is also excellent served in larger quantities as a main course.*

# Sweet Potato and Carrot Salad

*This salad has a sweet-and-sour taste, and can be served warm as part of a meal or eaten in a larger quantity as a main course.*

**SERVES 4**

INGREDIENTS

*1 medium sweet potato*
*2 carrots, cut into thick diagonal slices*
*3 medium tomatoes*
*8–10 iceberg lettuce leaves*
*75 g/3 oz/¹/₂ cup canned chick-peas
    (garbanzos), drained*

**Dressing**
*1 tbsp clear honey*
*6 tbsp natural (plain) low-fat yogurt*
*¹/₂ tsp salt*
*1 tsp coarsely ground black pepper*

**Garnish**
*1 tbsp walnuts*
*1 tbsp sultanas (golden raisins)*
*1 small onion, cut into rings*

| NUTRITIONAL VALUES (per portion) | |
| --- | --- |
| Total fat | 4.85 g |
| Saturated fat | 0.58 g |
| Cholesterol | 0.85 mg |
| Energy (kcals/kj) | 176/741 |

I ▲ Peel the sweet potato and roughly dice. Boil until soft but not mushy, cover the pan and set aside.

**2** Boil the carrots for a just a few minutes making sure they remain crunchy. Add the carrots to the sweet potatoes.

**3** ▲ Drain the water from the sweet potatoes and carrots and place together in a bowl.

**4** ▲ Slice the tops off the tomatoes, then scoop out and discard the seeds. Roughly chop the flesh.

**5** ▲ Line a glass bowl with the lettuce leaves. Mix together the sweet potatoes, carrots, chick-peas (garbanzos) and tomatoes and place in the bowl.

**6** ▲ Blend together all the dressing ingredients and beat using a fork.

**7** ▲ Garnish with the walnuts, sultanas (golden raisins) and onion rings. Pour the dressing over the salad or serve it in a separate bowl, if wished.

# Spinach and Mushroom Salad

*This salad is especially good served with the Glazed Garlic Prawns (Shrimp).*

**SERVES 4**

INGREDIENTS
*20 small spinach leaves*
*10 baby corn cobs*
*25 g/1 oz salad (garden) cress (optional)*
*115 g/4 oz/1 1/2 cups mushrooms*
*8–10 onion rings*
*2 medium tomatoes*
*salt*
*crushed black peppercorns*
*2 fresh coriander (cilantro) sprigs*
*   (optional)*
*3–4 lime slices (optional)*

| NUTRITIONAL VALUES (per portion) | |
| --- | --- |
| Total fat | 0.93 g |
| Saturated fat | 0.12 g |
| Cholesterol | 0.00 mg |
| Energy (kcals/kj) | 38/161 |

I ▲ Halve the baby corn cobs, and slice the mushrooms and tomatoes.

2 ▲ Arrange all the salad ingredients in a bowl. Season with salt and pepper and garnish with fresh coriander (cilantro) and lime slices, if wished.

# Nutty Salad

*A delicious and filling salad which can be served as an accompaniment or as an appetizer.*

**SERVES 4**

INGREDIENTS
*1 medium onion, cut into 12 rings*
*115 g/4 oz/1/2 cup canned red kidney*
*   beans, drained*
*1 medium green courgette (zucchini),*
*   sliced*
*1 medium yellow courgette, sliced*
*50 g/2 oz/2/3 cup pasta shells, cooked*
*50 g/2 oz/1/2 cup cashew nuts*
*25 g/1 oz/1/4 cup peanuts*

**Dressing**
*120 ml/4 fl oz/1/2 cup fromage frais*
*2 tbsp natural (plain) low-fat yogurt*
*1 fresh green chilli, chopped*
*1 tbsp chopped fresh coriander (cilantro)*
*1/2 tsp salt*
*1/2 tsp crushed black peppercorns*

*1/2 tsp crushed dried red chillies*
*1 tbsp lemon juice*
*lime wedges*

| NUTRITIONAL VALUES (per portion) | |
| --- | --- |
| Total fat | 7.14 g |
| Saturated fat | 1.09 g |
| Cholesterol | 0.56 mg |
| Energy (kcals/kj) | 153/642 |

I  Arrange the onion rings, red kidney beans, courgette (zucchini) slices and pasta in a salad dish and sprinkle the cashew nuts and peanuts over the top.

2 ▲ In a separate bowl, blend together the fromage frais, yogurt, green chilli, fresh coriander (cilantro) and salt and beat it well using a fork.

3  Sprinkle the black pepper, crushed red chillies and lemon juice over the dressing. Garnish the salad with the lime wedges and serve with the dressing in a separate bowl or poured over the salad.

*Spinach and Mushroom Salad (top) and Nutty Salad*

# Yogurt Salad

*A delicious salad with a yogurt base, this is really an Eastern version of coleslaw.*

**SERVES 4**

INGREDIENTS
*350 ml/12 fl oz/1½ cups natural (plain) low-fat yogurt*
*2 tsp clear honey*
*2 medium carrots, thickly sliced*
*2 spring onions (scallions), roughly chopped*
*115 g/4 oz/1½ cups cabbage, finely shredded*
*50 g/2 oz/⅓ cup sultanas (golden raisins)*
*50 g/2 oz/½ cup cashew nuts*
*16 white grapes, halved*
*½ tsp salt*
*1 tsp chopped fresh mint*
*3–4 mint sprigs (optional)*

| NUTRITIONAL VALUES (per portion) | |
| --- | --- |
| Total fat | 7.62 g |
| Saturated fat | 1.20 g |
| Cholesterol | 3.40 mg |
| Energy (kcals/kj) | 201/846 |

1 ▲ Using a fork, beat the yogurt in a bowl with the clear honey.

2 Mix together the carrots, spring onions (scallions), cabbage, sultanas (golden raisins), cashew nuts, grapes, salt and chopped mint.

3 ▲ Pour the yogurt mixture over the salad and blend everything together.

4 Transfer to a serving dish and garnish with the mint sprigs, if wished.

# Spicy Baby Vegetable Salad

*This warm vegetable salad makes an excellent accompaniment to almost any main course dish.*

**SERVES 6**

INGREDIENTS
*10 baby potatoes, halved*
*15 baby carrots*
*10 baby courgettes (zucchini)*
*115 g/4 oz/1½ cups button mushrooms*

**Dressing**
*3 tbsp lemon juice*
*1½ tbsp olive oil*
*1 tbsp chopped fresh coriander (cilantro)*
*1 tsp salt*
*2 small fresh green chillies, finely chopped*

| NUTRITIONAL VALUES (per portion) | |
| --- | --- |
| Total fat | 3.54 g |
| Saturated fat | 0.48 g |
| Cholesterol | 0.00 mg |
| Energy (kcals/kj) | 76/319 |

1 Wash and boil all the baby vegetables until tender. Drain and place these in a serving dish.

2 ▲ In a separate bowl, mix together all the ingredients for the dressing.

3 Toss the vegetables in the dressing and serve.

*Yogurt Salad (top) and Spicy Baby Vegetable Salad*

*Opposite: A market stall selling ripe and green bananas*
*Above: A street-trader offers fresh lemons*

# Desserts & Drinks

*Indian desserts are renowned for being very sweet and calorific, but with some simple adaptations authentic recipes such as Vermicelli and Ground Rice Pudding can be enjoyed without guilt. Or try Melon and Strawberry Salad for a delightfully refreshing end to an Indian meal. Lassi and Almond Sherbet are popular traditional drinks and, served chilled, are cooling to the palate.*

# Ground Rice Pudding

*This delicious and light ground rice pudding is the perfect end to a spicy meal. It can be served hot or cold.*

**SERVES 4–6**

INGREDIENTS
*50 g/2 oz/¹/₂ cup coarsely ground rice*
*25 g/1 oz/2 tbsp ground almonds*
*4 green cardamom pods, crushed*
*900 ml/1¹/₂ pints/3³/₄ cups semi-skimmed (2%) milk*
*6 tbsp sugar*
*1 tbsp rose water*

**Garnish**
*1 tbsp crushed pistachio nuts*
*silver leaf (varq) (optional)*

| NUTRITIONAL VALUES (per portion) | |
|---|---|
| Total fat | 8.78 g |
| Saturated fat | 2.57 g |
| Cholesterol | 14.70 mg |
| Energy (kcals/kj) | 201/844 |

2 ▲ Add the remaining milk and cook over a medium heat for about 10 minutes or until the rice mixture thickens to the consistency of a creamy chicken soup.

3 Stir in the sugar and rose water and continue to cook for a further 2 minutes. Serve garnished with pistachio nuts and silver leaf, if wished.

I ▲ Place the ground rice and almonds in a saucepan with the green cardamoms. Add 600 ml/1 pint/2½ cups milk and bring to the boil over a medium heat, stirring occasionally.

# Vermicelli

*Indian vermicelli, made from wheat, is much finer than Italian vermicelli and is readily available from Asian stores.*

**SERVES 4**

INGREDIENTS
*115 g/4 oz/1 cup vermicelli*
*1.2 litres/2 pints/5 cups water*
*¹/₂ tsp saffron strands*
*1 tbsp sugar*
*4 tbsp low-fat fromage frais (optional)*

**Garnish**
*1 tbsp shredded fresh coconut, or desiccated (shredded) coconut*
*1 tbsp flaked (slivered) almonds*
*1 tbsp chopped pistachio nuts*
*1 tbsp sugar*

| NUTRITIONAL VALUES (per portion) | |
|---|---|
| Total fat | 4.61 g |
| Saturated fat | 1.66 g |
| Cholesterol | 0.15 mg |
| Energy (kcals/kj) | 319/1341 |

2 ▲ Stir in the sugar and continue cooking until the water has evaporated. Strain through a sieve (strainer), if necessary, to remove any excess liquid.

3 Place the vermicelli in a serving dish and garnish with the shredded coconut, almonds, pistachio nuts and sugar. Serve with fromage frais, if wished.

I ▲ Crush the vermicelli in your hands and place in a saucepan. Pour in the water, add the saffron and bring to the boil. Boil for about 5 minutes.

*Ground Rice Pudding (top) and Vermicelli*

# Melon and Strawberry Salad

*A beautiful and colourful fruit salad, this is suitable to serve as a refreshing appetizer or to round off a meal.*

**SERVES 4**

INGREDIENTS
*1 galia melon*
*1 honeydew melon*
*½ watermelon*
*225 g/8 oz fresh strawberries*
*1 tbsp lemon juice*
*1 tbsp clear honey*
*1 tbsp chopped fresh mint*
*1 mint sprig (optional)*

| NUTRITIONAL VALUES (per portion) | |
| --- | --- |
| Total fat | 0.84 g |
| Saturated fat | 0.00 g |
| Cholesterol | 0.00 mg |
| Energy (kcals/kj) | 139/584 |

1 ▲ Prepare the melons by cutting them in half and discarding the seeds. Use a melon baller to scoop out the flesh into balls or a knife to cut it into cubes. Place these in a fruit bowl.

2 Rinse and take the stems off the strawberries, cut these in half and add them to the fruit bowl.

3 ▲ Mix together the lemon juice and clear honey and add about 1 tbsp of water to make this easier to pour over the fruit. Mix into the fruit gently.

4 ▲ Sprinkle the chopped mint over the top of the fruit. Serve garnished with the mint sprig, if wished.

**COOK'S TIP**

*Use whichever melons are available: replace galia with cantaloupe or watermelon with charentais, for example. Try to choose three melons with a variation in colour for an attractive effect.*

# Caramel with Fresh Fruit

*A creamy caramel dessert is a wonderful way to end a meal. It is light and delicious, and this recipe is very simple.*

## SERVES 6

### INGREDIENTS
**Caramel**
*2 tbsp sugar*
*2 tbsp water*

**Custard**
*6 medium eggs*
*4 drops vanilla essence (extract)*
*8–10 tbsp sugar*
*750 ml/1¼ pints/good 3 cups semi-skimmed (2%) milk*
*fresh fruit for serving*

| NUTRITIONAL VALUES (per portion) | |
| --- | --- |
| Total fat | 7.40 g |
| Saturated fat | 2.77 g |
| Cholesterol | 201.25 mg |
| Energy (kcals/kj) | 229/964 |

1  To make the caramel, place the sugar and water in a heatproof dish and place in a microwave and cook for 4 minutes on high or until the sugar has caramelized. Or melt in a pan until pale gold in colour. Pour into a 1.2 litre/2 pint/5 cup soufflé dish. Leave to cool.

2 ▲ Preheat the oven to 180°C/350°F/ Gas 4. To make the custard, break the eggs into a medium mixing bowl and whisk until frothy.

3 ▲ Stir in the vanilla essence (extract) and gradually add the sugar then the milk, whisking continuously.

4 ▲ Pour the custard over the top of the caramel.

5  Cook in the preheated oven for 35–40 minutes. Remove from the oven and leave to cool for about 30 minutes or until set.

6  Loosen the custard from the sides of the dish with a knife. Place a serving dish upside-down on top of the soufflé dish and invert, giving a gentle shake.

7  Arrange any fruit of your choice around the caramel and serve. Strawberries, blueberries, orange rings, banana slices and raspberries form the colourful array shown here.

# Lassi

*Lassi is a very popular drink both in India and Pakistan. It is available not only from roadside cafés but is also a great favourite in good restaurants and hotels. There is no substitute for this drink, especially on a hot day. It is ideal served with hot dishes as it helps the body to digest spicy food.*

**SERVES 4**

**INGREDIENTS**
*300 ml/¹/₂ pint/1¹/₄ cups natural (plain) low-fat yogurt*
*1 tsp sugar, or to taste*
*300 ml/¹/₂ pint/1¹/₄ cups water*
*2 tbsp puréed fruit (optional)*
*1 tbsp crushed pistachio nuts*

| NUTRITIONAL VALUES (per portion) | |
| --- | --- |
| Total fat | 1.91 g |
| Saturated fat | 0.52 g |
| Cholesterol | 2.80 mg |
| Energy (kcals/kj) | 60/251 |

2 ▲ Pour in the water and the puréed fruit, if using, and continue to whisk for 2 minutes.

3  Pour the lassi into serving glasses. Serve chilled, decorated with crushed pistachio nuts.

1 ▲ Place the yogurt in a jug and whisk it for about 2 minutes until frothy. Add the sugar to taste.

# Almond Sherbert

*Traditionally this drink was always made in the month of Ramaden, when we used to break our fast. It should be served chilled.* ·

**SERVES 4**

**INGREDIENTS**
*50 g/2 oz/¹/₂ cup ground almonds*
*600 ml/1 pint/2¹/₂ cups semi-skimmed (2%) milk*
*2 tsp sugar, or to taste*

| NUTRITIONAL VALUES (per portion) | |
| --- | --- |
| Total fat | 6.15 g |
| Saturated fat | 1.70 g |
| Cholesterol | 9.80 mg |
| Energy (kcals/kj) | 117/492 |

2 ▲ Pour in the milk and sugar and stir to mix. Taste for sweetness and serve chilled.

1 ▲ Put the ground almonds into a jug.

*Lassi flavoured with puréed raspberries (left) and Almond Sherbert*

# Index